God Speaks, Are You Listening?

A Twelve Week Discipleship Bible Study

Christine Cloninger

God Speaks, Are You Listening?: A Twelve Week Discipleship Bible Study
Copyright © 2024 Christine Cloninger and Becoming Whole in Christ (BWIC) Ministries
Revised Edition of "Becoming Whole In Christ" by same author New Last Name. Copyright © 2012. www.bwicministries.com.

Edited and proofread by: Katelyn Silva, We Write Books
Cover and Interior Design by: Katelyn Silva, We Write Books

ISBN (paperback, bundle): 979-8-9905662-8-6
ISBN (paperback, vol. 1): 978-1-965652-42-8
ISBN (paperback, vol. 2): 978-1-965652-43-5

Printed in the United States of America.

All rights reserved. No part of this book reproduced by any means, electronic or mechanical, including photocopying, recording, or by any information storage retrieval system, without permission of the copyright owner, except for the inclusion of brief quotations for a review.

Scripture quotations noted NIV are from the LIFE APPLICATION BIBLE: NEW INTERNATIONAL VERSION® Copyright © 1988, 1989, 1990, 1991 by Tyndale House Publishers, Inc. Wheaton, IL 60189. All rights reserved.

How to Hear God's Voice material used with the permission of Communing with God Ministries and President, Mark Virkler. For additional resources and more information on this ministry/online university, go to www.CWGministries.org or www.cluonline.com

The accountability questions were used with the permission of Character that Counts and Rod Handley. For added resources and more information on this ministry go to: www.characterthatcounts.org

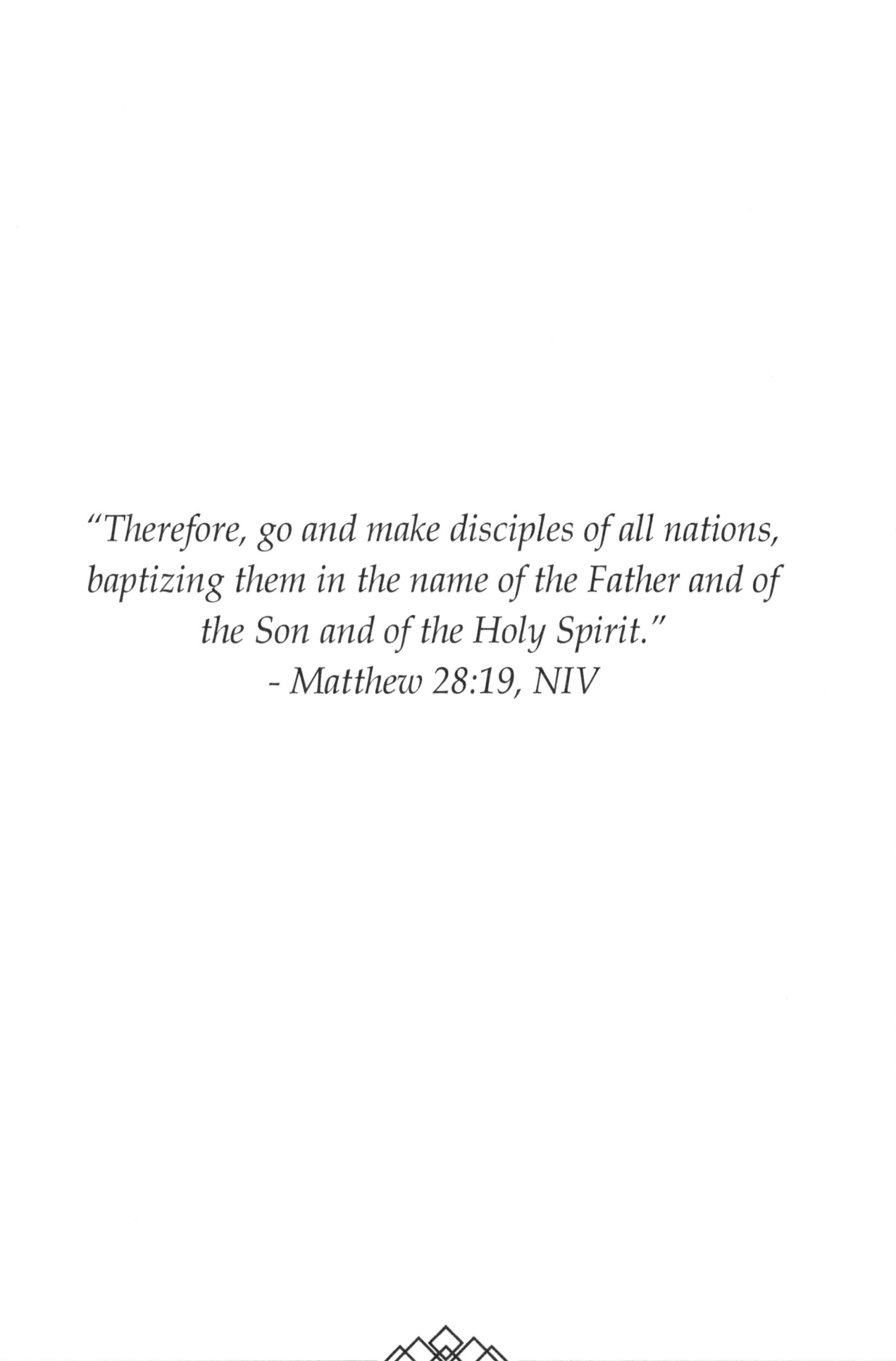

"Therefore, go and make disciples of all nations, baptizing them in the name of the Father and of the Son and of the Holy Spirit."
- Matthew 28:19, NIV

Contents

Acknowledgments

I want to thank my Heavenly Father for placing the desire in my heart to put this study together. May He receive the GLORY for any changes made in people's lives as they are going through it!

Thanks to *all* the people who encouraged me, mentored me, taught me, and helped me along the way in producing this Twelve Week Discipleship Bible Study. May God bless each one of you in a personal and powerful way!

Foreword

God speaks through experiences we have, movies we watch, songs we hear, things we do, people in our lives, events that happen, that still small voice, and His Word. If we learn to listen, we can learn to hear when God speaks.

Tuesday, August 9, 2011, **90 Days of Discovery**

My true soul sister, Linda, is the one who taught me how to open the lid of the small box I had placed God in. This allowed His divine Holy Spirit, 16 years ago, to flow into my life and fill my very being! During part of those years, for reason unknown to us, God placed Linda and her family in California. She is back now, and together we have experienced a journey like no other.

While in California, Linda met Christine. In obedience to God's pressing, Christine wrote an intense Bible study. Christine contacted Linda and asked if she would be willing to obtain an accountability partner to do the study as a preview before it was published. Linda understood that she and her partner would vigilantly go through the daily assignments. One assignment was to meet and discuss the lessons. Having accepted the quest, Linda chose me as her study, prayer, and accountability partner. We began the process with a careful dissection of the introduction. I made up my mind from the get-go that if I was going to commit myself, I was going to absorb every single word. The introduction was just as powerful as the study itself. Along the way, we let Christine know our progress and thoughts.

It is tough to decide what part of this study is my favorite. I enjoyed the mornings alone with God when my house was either asleep or empty. I learned how to journal by hearing my Creator and what He was speaking in my life. The Holy Spirit prompted and gave me the material to write a lesson on becoming acquainted with Him. I discovered and grew in the different sides of my life in which the study addresses. I especially enjoyed the sweet early Saturday mornings when Linda and I escaped to the coffee shop and cuddled up in the soft corner chairs we dubbed as our "assigned seats." We would unravel all the amazing things God so sweetly exposed to us during the week. Another favorite thing was the growth and depth of my prayer life. It truly was the culmination of all these blessings combined. What we have learned and experienced has not simply stayed between Linda and me. No, it has expounded out, causing a ripple effect in our lives and the lives of those around us! Prayers answered and voyages began.

I have been able to use things I have discovered through this study in my job. Linda has been able to do wonderful things in her job, as well. It was for such an effect as this that God had placed the Jones family in California.

I thought it was next to impossible that Linda and I could get any closer as soul sisters, but God spoke through her those sixteen years ago when she taught me. He spoke to her husband when they moved out of state. He spoke when Linda and Christine met. He spoke when He prompted Christine to write His Bible study. He spoke when Linda chose me to do this with her. He spoke every single day over the last few sessions. He is always there, and it is through listening and obedience that we know when God speaks.

– Treva

Introduction

It's best to start this discipleship bible study in a small group of 3 – 4 attendees or with an accountability partner, not alone. If you decide to do this on your own, you will experience things as you go through the study that other people may not understand because they are not learning what you are learning. So, make it a point to do this journey with someone. You can meet each other weekly in person, via e-mail, or phone call. When you come together, take time to share what God is showing you in the Scriptures and answer any questions that you may have. Recite the memorized verse(s), testify what God is doing in your life, take prayer requests and go through accountability questions (See Appendices).

STOP!
Pray for God to reveal who this person will be for the rest of your discipleship journey. This person can celebrate with you, pray with you, and encourage you, especially during difficult times of spiritual attacks.

Accountability/Prayer Partner's Name: _____

———————◆———————

By sharing what you learn and experience with your accountability partner or small group, it can help bring balance in five major areas of your life: spiritual, mental, social/emotional, physical, and financial. During your time in God's Word, you will learn you are a child of God and He loves you unconditionally. As you go through each lesson, take in *all* God want to teach you so you can be effective in sharing His love with others. Learn God's Word, live it out, and lead others to it! That is discipleship. And a disciple is a disciplined learner. They take their time to understand, apply, and be changed by the Word of God. My prayer is that once you have completed the journey with God, your walk with Him will be much stronger, and you will be able to hear when He speaks to you.

I recommend taking a weekend or even a preparation week to set goals to work on through the study and dig in to understanding the areas of discipline. By doing so, you will establish a strong foundation and prepare for God's work in your life.

Your personal journey will be altogether unique compared to anyone else, because everyone is in a different place in their walk with the Lord. You may be a person that is curious about who this Jesus is, someone who has recently drifted away from God, someone who just needs to strengthen their walk with Jesus, or one who wants to lead others on their journey. Wherever you are, take this journey with an open mind and dedication. Stay committed to the end, and your life can be transformed. May you experience newness in your perspectives, be encouraged in your daily walk with God, and have a greater understanding of His loving presence. May the Lord bless you greatly as you search for answers!

To begin this journey with God, write down where you currently are in your life. Jot down any activities that come to mind that you are involved in doing. (Examples: Going to school, working at…, volunteering for…, names of close friends…, outdoor and indoor activities.)

Fill out the Initial Self-Evaluation on the next page to see what you are currently doing in each of the five areas discussed in the study. Answer the questions honestly. At the end of the study, you will be given the opportunity to retake the Self-Evaluation again to see where there has been positive change in your life. My prayer is that there will be a noticeable change.

Initial Self-Evaluation

To get a larger, printable download of the Self-Evaluation to use again anytime you like, go to bwicministries.com/evaluation.

My life as of _____, 20_____

Spiritual	Yes	No	How Often
Do I read God's Word each day?			
Do I pray for my family, others, and myself?			
Am I attending a Bible-based Church?			
Do I testify about God to others?			
Mental			
Do I have a cheerful outlook?			
Do I listen to, watch, and read things that are uplifting and encouraging?			
Do I speak and react to others in a kind manner?			
Social/Emotional			
Do I honor and respect my spouse and family?			
Am I learning from a mentor or coach?			
Am I involved in a small group/community?			
Physical			
Do I eat/drink the right things each day?			
Do I exercise every day?			
Do I get enough rest daily?			
Financial			
Do I give to the Lord?			
Am I in debt?			
Do I save for an emergency fund?			
Total of columns			

STOP!
Do Not Read any further until you have completed the Initial Self-Evaluation.

Life Disciplines

Let us begin our journey by looking at each of the five areas of discipline: spiritual, mental, social/emotional, physical, and financial.

Spiritual

Contemplating a walk with the Lord is a journey of the soul. The Bible says in 1 Cor. 6 :19, "…For we are the temple of the living God." As God has said, 'I will live with them and walk among them, and I will be their God, and they will be my people'" (II Corinthians 6:16b).

Learning to trust the Lord with your desires, pondering the possibility of an intimate friendship with someone you cannot see, and finding answers to your spiritual questions is a lifetime progression. But it all begins with a personal relationship with Jesus.

A Personal Relationship with Jesus

As you read this section, take time to look up every verse mentioned from the Bible. You might want to consider highlighting, underlining, or marking these verses in your Bible to have available when sharing the gospel with new believers.

Having a relationship with Jesus means trusting Him with your whole life. Some of you may think that because you go to church you have this relationship with him, but that may not be the case, even if you were brought up in a family that went on a regular basis. Going to church will not save you, but it can lead to a journey of knowing who Jesus is and what He has done.

Everyone must walk their own journey of faith in Jesus Christ. He, with the power of the Holy Spirit, will teach you and help you understand the Bible. "The man without the Spirit does not accept the things that come from the Spirit of God, for they are foolishness to him, and he cannot understand them because they are spiritually discerned" (I Corinthians 2:14). This verse means to understand God's Word, you must ask Jesus to come into your heart through the indwelling of the Holy Spirit. Having this personal relationship with Jesus will bring a new perspective on spiritual things.

Our culture, today, has made sin a commonplace and we sometimes do not recognize our own sin. However, in Romans 3:23, it says, "…all have sinned and fall short of the glory of God." We were all born into this fallen world. There is nothing you can do to save yourself. "For the wages of sin is death, but the gift of God is eternal life in Christ Jesus our Lord" (Romans 6:23).

What is eternal life? "This is eternal life: that they may know You, The Only True God, and Jesus Christ, whom You have sent" (John 17:3). God's love for you is eternal. Jesus Christ died on the cross to pay the penalty for all your sins. "God demonstrates His own love for us in this: while we were still sinners, Christ died for us" (Romans 5:8).

Because of His grace and mercy, God forgives <u>ALL</u> your sins: past, present, and future. "Therefore, since we have been justified through faith, we have peace with God through our Lord Jesus Christ" (Romans 5:1). "If you confess with your mouth, 'Jesus is Lord,' and believe in your heart that God raised Him from the dead, you will be saved. For it is with your heart that you believe and are justified, and it is with your mouth that you confess and are saved" (Romans 10:9-10). Therefore, there is no condemnation for those who are in Christ Jesus" (Romans 8:1).

"For I am convinced that neither death nor life, neither angels nor demons, neither the present nor the future, nor any powers, neither height or depth, nor anything else in all creation will be able to separate us from the love of God that is in Christ Jesus our Lord" (Romans 8:38-39). AMEN!

You might be wondering, "How do I apply this truth to my life?" The answer is P.R.A.Y! *Information taken from the National Day of Prayer Pamphlet.

Praise... expressing warm appreciation for what God has already done through Jesus.

"God made Him who had no sin to be sin for us, so that in Him we might become the righteousness of God" (II Corinthians 5:21). Through our Lord and friend, Jesus, God became our Father. Jesus died on the cross on your behalf.

The death of Jesus made your salvation possible. Jesus said in John 14:6, "I am The Way, The Truth, and The Life! No one comes to The Father except through Me."

Repent... turn from your sinful ways by confessing your sins and place your focus on God. Sin is anything you think, say, or do that goes against the Word of God, or anything that takes precedence over Jesus in your life. Other examples of sin include lust of the eyes, lust of the flesh, and pride of life. A truly repentant heart will feel conviction like Isaiah who said, "Woe is me...I am ruined! For I am a man of unclean lips..." (Isaiah 6:5a)

Take time now to confess any of your sins, and allow your heart, mind, and soul to be renewed by God. The Lord is quick to forgive when we come to Him.

> He, (God) does not treat us as our sins deserve or repay us according to our iniquities. For as high as the heavens are above the earth, so great is His love for those who fear Him, as far as the east is from the west, so far has He removed our transgressions from us? (Emphasis added, Psalm 103:10-12)

Ask… allow God to reveal His truth, turn your heart back to Him, and bring healing as you ask Him to purify your life.

> Submit yourselves, then, to God. Resist the Devil, and he will flee from you. Come near to God and He will come near to you. Wash your hands… and purify your hearts… Humble yourselves before the Lord, and He will lift you up. (James 4:7-8, 10)

Yield… by surrendering to the Lord and recognizing He has heard your prayers and will answer according to His will. He is waiting to supply guidance and direction!

> If you confess with your mouth, 'Jesus is Lord.' and believe in your heart that God raised him from the dead, you will be saved. For it is with your heart that you believe and are justified, and it is with your mouth that you confess and are saved… For everyone who calls on the name of the Lord will be saved. (Romans 10:9-10, 13)

Trust God to make the needed changes in your life through the power of Holy Spirit. Believe He has your best interest in mind. Listen for the voice of God to strengthen you through the written Word of God and prayer.

STOP!
If you have not given your life to the Lord and received Jesus Christ as your Lord and Savior…
Honestly mean it from your heart as you pray, and you will be saved!

Lord Jesus, I know that I am a sinner. Without You in my life, I have nothing. You came down from heaven to save me from my sins and are now sitting at the right hand of God, the Father, interceding on my behalf. Help me turn from my sins. I choose to follow You for the rest of my life. Change me from the inside out. Let me be a bold witness for You. I surrender my life into Your hands, in Jesus' Holy and Precious Name, Amen! How do you know you are saved? I John 5:13 says, "I write these things to you who believe in the name of the Son of God so that you may know that you have eternal life."

If you have just received Jesus Christ, the angels in heaven are singing and rejoicing over you right now. You are now a child of God! I am excited for you. Tell someone what God has just done for you. He has saved you and forgiven you.

As you follow Jesus more closely, you will know what He is saying. Ask Him for wisdom and trust. "…wisdom that comes from heaven is first of all pure, then peace-loving, considerate, submissive, full of mercy, and good fruit, impartial and sincere" (James 3:17).

The Holy Spirit will teach you through God's Word everything you need to know. Meditate on what He is teaching you. Ask yourself, "What do I need to change in my life to apply this newfound truth?" With Christ living in your heart, rely on the Holy Spirit to bring change and wholeness into your life.

A Special Time with God

God should be the most important person in your life. He wants to spend time with you daily. He will wait for you. Make it a priority to meet with Him every day. Make it a date, not a ritual! Take advantage of this opportunity. Keep this intimate time with Him. He is your best friend. Make this a normal activity. If this is new to you, give it time; it can become a natural part of your life. Life may get in the way, but remember the Bible says, "… seek first His Kingdom and His Righteousness…" (Matthew 6:33a)

I believe, with all my heart, the *most important* thing you can do is have a consistent daily time with God. It will take time and effort to begin to see the spiritual side of who God is. Little strides are commendable. As Jesus said, "Whoever can be trusted with very little can also be trusted with much" (Luke 16:10a).

By walking with God daily, the spiritual fruit produced are "…love, joy, peace, patience, kindness, goodness, faithfulness, gentleness, and self-control" (Galatians 5:22-23a).

Pray For Family, Others, and Yourself

Prayer is a two-way communication with GOD, the One who loves you. Talk to Him about everything and anything. It does not matter where you are. It could be in the shower, on your knees, in your car (eyes open if driving, of course), as you take a walk. He will talk to you by the Holy Spirit in different ways. Be still before Him and sit at His feet. If you take time to listen, He can even speak to you through nature.

When you pray, do not just ask for things. God is not in the business of giving you everything you want. He will give you what is best for you now. He may say, "YES, you can have that," "NO, that would not be good for you," or "WAIT, you are not ready to manage what you are asking." When told to wait, it may be the hardest thing to do. God may need to build your character to match your new responsibility.

Until you enter heaven, answered prayers may never happen, but be persistent. "The prayer of a righteous man is powerful and effective" (James 5:16b).

As I was collaborating with my mother, Pat Callado, in putting this study together, she shared how God Almighty spoke to her as she gave Him her full attention by listening to Him when she prayed. This is what she experienced.

> "I wanted to search my heart, mind, soul, spirit, will, and emotions to clear any residue from this clay pot that I am. I asked God to cleanse everything known and unknown to make me a shiny, luminous, receptive temple of the Holy Spirit. No closed doors or kept desires; no thoughts of I, me, or mine left. The spiritual eyesight I received is difficult to explain. I had prayed constantly for two years for an answer to a special prayer and had been very frustrated by no answer. In my weakness over it, the Lord spiritually showed me a stainless-steel door that reached from Earth to

Heaven. He asked me to help Him close that door, and I did. He then told me everything behind the door belonged to Him. The Lord then showed me the pieces of a puzzle on a table. Before completing a picture, every piece had to fit into place. Meaning prayer indeed changes things, but He has pieces to play before it all fits into His divine plan. Other lives are also involved. Moreover, like puzzle pieces, fall on the floor."

How to Hear God's Voice – From Dr. Mark Virkler

She had done it again! Instead of coming straight home from school like she was supposed to, she had gone to her friend's house. Without permission. Without our knowledge. Without doing her chores.

With a ministering household that included remnants of three struggling families plus our own toddler and newborn, my wife simply couldn't handle all the work on her own. Everyone had to pull their own weight. Everyone had age-appropriate tasks they were expected to complete.

At fourteen, Rachel and her younger brother were living with us while her parents tried to overcome lifestyle patterns that had resulted in the children running away to escape the dysfunction. I felt sorry for Rachel, but, honestly, my wife was my greatest concern.

Now Rachel had ditched her chores to spend time with her friends. It wasn't the first time, but if I had anything to say about it, it would be the last. I intended to lay down the law when she got home and make it very clear that if she was going to live under my roof, she would obey my rules.

But…she wasn't home yet. And I had recently been learning to hear God's voice more clearly. Maybe I should try to see if I could hear anything from Him about the situation. Maybe He could give me a way to get her to do what she was supposed to (i.e. what I wanted her to do).

So I went to my office and reviewed what the Lord had been teaching me from Habakkuk 2:1,2: "I will stand on my guard post and station myself on the rampart; And I will keep watch to see what He will speak to me…Then the Lord answered me and said, 'Record the vision….'"

Habakkuk said, "I will stand on my guard post..." (Hab. 2:1).

Key #1 - The first key to hearing God's voice is to go to a quiet place and still our own thoughts and emotions.

Psalm 46:10 encourages us to be still, let go, cease striving, and know that He is God. In Psalm 37:7 we are called to "be still before the Lord and wait patiently for Him." There is a deep inner knowing in our spirits that each of us can experience when we quiet our flesh and our minds. Practicing the art of biblical meditation helps silence the outer noise and distractions clamoring for our attention.

I didn't have a guard post, but I did have an office, so I went there to quiet my temper and my mind. Loving God through a quiet worship song is one very effective way to become still. In 2

Kings 3, Elisha needed a word from the Lord so he said, "Bring me a minstrel," and as the minstrel played, the Lord spoke. I have found that playing a worship song on my autoharp is the quickest way for me to come to stillness. I need to choose my song carefully; boisterous songs of praise do not bring me to stillness, but rather gentle songs that express my love and worship. And it isn't enough just to sing the song into the cosmos – I come into the Lord's presence most quickly and easily when I use my godly imagination to see the truth that He is right here with me and I sing my songs to Him, personally.

"I will keep watch to see," said the prophet. To receive the pure word of God, it is very important that my heart be properly focused as I become still, because my focus is the source of the intuitive flow. If I fix my eyes upon Jesus (Heb. 12:2), the intuitive flow comes from Jesus. But if I fix my gaze upon some desire of my heart, the intuitive flow comes out of that desire. To have a pure flow I must become still and carefully fix my eyes upon Jesus. Quietly worshiping the King and receiving out of the stillness that follows quite easily accomplishes this.

So, I used **the second key to hearing God's voice:**

Key #2 - As you pray, fix the eyes of your heart upon Jesus, seeing in the Spirit the dreams and visions of Almighty God.

Habakkuk was looking for vision as he prayed. He opened the eyes of his heart and looked into the spirit world to see what God wanted to show him. God has always spoken through dreams and visions, and He specifically said that they would come to those upon whom the Holy Spirit is poured out (Acts 2:1-4, 17).

Being a logical, rational person, observable facts that could be verified by my physical senses were the foundations of my life, including my spiritual life. I had never thought of opening the eyes of my heart and looking for vision. However, I have come to believe that this is exactly what God wants me to do. He gave me eyes in my heart to see in the spirit the vision and movement of Almighty God. There is an active spirit world all around us, full of angels, demons, the Holy Spirit, the omnipresent Father, and His omnipresent Son, Jesus. The only reasons for me not to see this reality are unbelief or lack of knowledge.

In his sermon in Acts 2:25, Peter refers to King David's statement: "I saw the Lord always in my presence; for He is at my right hand, so that I will not be shaken." The original psalm makes it clear that this was a decision of David's, not a constant supernatural visitation: "I have set (literally, I have placed) the Lord continually before me; because He is at my right hand, I will not be shaken" (Ps.16:8). Because David knew that the Lord was always with him, he determined in his spirit to *see* that truth with the eyes of his heart as he went through life, knowing that this would keep his faith strong.

To see, we must look. Daniel saw a vision in his mind and said, "I was looking...I kept looking...I kept looking" (Dan. 7:2, 9, 13). As I pray, I look for Jesus, and I watch as He speaks to me, doing and saying the things that are on His heart. Many Christians will find that if they only look, they will see. Jesus is Emmanuel, God with us (Matt. 1:23). It is as simple as that. You can see Christ present with you because Christ *is* present with you. In fact, the vision may come so easily that you will be tempted to reject it, thinking that it is just you. But if you persist in recording these visions, your doubt will soon be overcome by faith as you recognize that the content of them could only be birthed in Almighty God.

Jesus demonstrated the ability of living out of constant contact with God, declaring that He did nothing on His own initiative, but only what He saw the Father doing, and heard the Father saying (Jn. 5:19,20,30). What an incredible way to live!

Is it possible for us to live out of divine initiative as Jesus did? Yes! We must simply fix our eyes upon Jesus. The veil has been torn, giving access into the immediate presence of God, and He calls us to draw near (Lk. 23:45; Heb. 10:19-22). "I pray that the eyes of your heart will be enlightened…."

When I had quieted my heart enough that I was able to picture Jesus without the distractions of my own ideas and plans, I was able to "keep watch to see what He will speak to me." I wrote down my question: "Lord, what should I do about Rachel?"

Immediately the thought came to me, "She is insecure." Well, that certainly wasn't my thought! Her behavior looked like a rebellion to me, not insecurity.

But like Habakkuk, I was coming to know the sound of God speaking to me (Hab. 2:2). Elijah described it as a still, small voice (I Kings 19:12). I had previously listened for an inner audible voice, and God does speak that way at times. However, I have found that usually, God's voice comes as spontaneous thoughts, visions, feelings, or impressions.

For example, haven't you been driving down the road and had a thought come to you to pray for a certain person? Didn't you believe it was God telling you to pray? What did God's voice sound like? Was it an audible voice, or was it a spontaneous thought that lit upon your mind?

Experience indicates that we perceive spirit-level communication as spontaneous thoughts, impressions and visions, and Scripture confirms this in many ways. For example, one definition of *paga*, a Hebrew word for intercession, is "a chance encounter or an accidental intersecting." When God lays people on our hearts, He does it through *paga*, a chance-encounter thought "accidentally" intersecting our minds.

Key #3 - The third key to hearing God's voice is recognizing that God's voice in your heart often sounds like a flow of spontaneous thoughts.

Therefore, when I want to hear from God, I tune to chance-encounter or spontaneous thoughts.

Finally, God told Habakkuk to record the vision (Hab. 2:2). This was not an isolated command. The Scriptures record many examples of individual's prayers and God's replies, such as the Psalms, many of the prophets, and Revelation. I have found that obeying this final principle amplified my confidence in my ability to hear God's voice so that I could finally make living out of His initiatives a way of life.

Key #4 - The fourth key, two-way journaling or the writing out of your prayers and God's answers, brings great freedom in hearing God's voice.

I have found two-way journaling to be a fabulous catalyst for clearly discerning God's inner, spontaneous flow, because as I journal, I am able to write in faith for long periods of time, simply believing it is God. I know that what I believe I have received from God must be tested. However, testing involves doubt and doubt blocks divine communication, so I do not want to test while I am trying to receive. (See James 1:5-8.) With journaling, I can receive in faith, knowing that when the flow has ended, I can test and examine it carefully.

So I wrote down what I believed He had said: "She is insecure."

But the Lord wasn't done. I continued to write the spontaneous thoughts that came to me: "Love her unconditionally. She is flesh of your flesh and bone of your bone."

My mind immediately objected: She is not flesh of my flesh. She is not related to me at all – she is a foster child, just living in my home temporarily. It was time to test this "word from the Lord"!

There are three possible sources of thoughts in our minds: ourselves, satan and the Holy Spirit. It was obvious that the words in my journal did not come from my own mind – I certainly didn't see her as insecure *or* flesh of my flesh. And I sincerely doubted that satan would encourage me to love anyone unconditionally!

Okay, it was starting to look like I might have received counsel from the Lord. It was consistent with the names and character of God as revealed in the Scripture, and totally contrary to the names and character of the enemy. So that meant that I was hearing from the Lord, and He wanted me to see the situation in a different light. Rachel was my daughter – part of my family not by blood but by the hand of God Himself. The chaos of her birth home had created deep insecurity about her worthiness to be loved by anyone, including me and including God. Only the unconditional love of the Lord expressed through an imperfect human would reach her heart.

But there was still one more test I needed to perform before I would have absolute confidence that this was truly God's word to me: I needed confirmation from someone else whose spiritual discernment I trusted. So, I went to see my wife and shared what I had received. I knew if I could get her validation, especially since she was the one most wronged in the situation, then I could say, at least to myself, "Thus sayeth the Lord."

Patti immediately and without question confirmed that the Lord had spoken to me. My entire planned lecture was forgotten. I returned to my office anxious to hear more. As the Lord planted a new, supernatural love for Rachel within me, He showed me what to say and how to say it to not only address the current issue of household responsibility, but the deeper issues of love and acceptance and worthiness.

Rachel and her brother remained as part of our family for another two years, giving us many opportunities to demonstrate and teach about Father's love, planting spiritual seeds in thirsty soil.

We weren't perfect and we didn't solve all her issues, but because I had learned to listen to the Lord, we were able to avoid creating more brokenness and separation.

The four simple keys that the Lord showed me from Habakkuk have been used by people of all ages, from four to a hundred and four, from every continent, culture and denomination, to break through into intimate two-way conversations with their loving Father and dearest Friend. Omitting any one of the keys will prevent you from receiving all He wants to say to you. The order of the keys is not important, just that you *use them all*. Embracing all four, by faith, can change your life. Simply quiet yourself down, tune to spontaneity, look for vision, and journal. He is waiting to meet you there.

You will be amazed when you journal! Doubt may hinder you at first, but throw it off, reminding yourself that it is a biblical concept, and that God is present, speaking to His children. Relax. When we cease our labors and enter His rest, God is free to flow (Heb. 4:10).

Why not try it for yourself, right now? Sit back comfortably, take out your pen and paper, and smile. Turn your attention toward the Lord in praise and worship, seeking His face. Many people have found the music and visionary prayer called "A Stroll Along the Sea of Galilee" helpful in getting them started. You can listen to it and download it for free at: www.CWGMinistries.org/Galilee.

After you write your question to Him, become still, fixing your gaze on Jesus. You will suddenly have a very good thought. Don't doubt it; simply write it down. Later, as you read your journaling, you, too, will be blessed to discover that you are indeed dialoguing with God. If you wonder if it is really the Lord speaking to you, share it with your spouse or a friend. Their input will encourage your faith and strengthen your commitment to spend time getting to know the Lover of your soul more intimately than you ever dreamed possible.

Is It *Really* God?

Five ways to be sure what you're hearing is from Him:

1) Test the Origin (1 Jn. 4:1)

Thoughts from our own minds are progressive, with one thought leading to the next, however tangentially. Thoughts from the spirit world are spontaneous. The Hebrew word for true prophecy is *naba,* which literally means to bubble up, whereas false prophecy is *ziyd* meaning to boil up. True words from the Lord will bubble up from our innermost being we don't need to cook them up ourselves.

2) Compare It to Biblical Principles

God will never say something to you personally which is contrary to His universal revelation as expressed in the Scriptures. If the Bible clearly states that something is a sin, no amount of journaling can make it right. Much of what you journal about will not be specifically addressed in the Bible, however, so an understanding of biblical principles is also needed.

3) Compare It to the Names and Character of God as Revealed in the Bible

Anything God says to you will be in harmony with His essential nature. Journaling will help you get to *know* God personally, but knowing what the Bible says *about* Him will help you discern what words are from Him. Make sure the tenor of your journaling lines up with the character of God as described in the names of the Father, Son and Holy Spirit.

4) Test the Fruit (Matt. 7:15-20)

What effect does what you are hearing have on your soul and your spirit? Words from the Lord will quicken your faith and increase your love, peace and joy. They will stimulate a sense of humility within you as you become more aware of Who God is and who you are. On the other hand, any words you receive which cause you to fear or doubt, which bring you into confusion or anxiety, or which stroke your ego (especially if you hear something that is "just for you alone – no one else is worthy") must be immediately rebuked and rejected as lies of the enemy.

5) Share It with Your Spiritual Counselors (Prov. 11:14)

We are members of a Body! A cord of three strands is not easily broken and God's intention has always been for us to grow together. Nothing will increase your faith in your ability to hear from God like having it confirmed by two or three other people! Share it with your spouse, your parents, your friends, your elder, your group leader, even your grown children can be your sounding board. They don't need to be perfect or super-spiritual; they just need to love you, be committed to being available to you, have a solid biblical orientation, and most importantly, they must also willingly and easily receive counsel. Avoid the authoritarian who insists that because of their standing in the church or with God, they no longer need to listen to others. Find two or three people and let them confirm that you are hearing from God!

To learn more, check out the book *4 Keys to Hearing God's Voice* at: www.cwgministries.org/4keys.

A Good Bible-Based Church

There are different churches and denominations in the world. Be sure the church you are attending or will attend teaches from the Word of God <u>only</u>. If they are not, then find another church. This is so important for your spiritual growth. If you need help finding a good Bible-based church, ask God to lead you to the right church. Trust me, He will. When you find a church, attend at least five times in a row to allow the Holy Spirit to confirm if this is the church for you.

Baptism

Baptism is an outward expression of your commitment to follow Jesus Christ. It doesn't save you but represents 'dying' with Christ in the water and being raised again to new life in Christ Jesus. **If you have never been baptized, now is the time to step out in obedience and do it!**

The Holy Spirit Responsibility

There are three different types of experiences a person will have from the Holy Spirit: with you, in you, and upon you. The first experience of the Holy Spirit is that He is with every person on the face of the earth. He comes alongside a person, nudging them to accept Jesus Christ as their Lord and Savior.

The second experience from the Holy Spirit is a one-time occurrence at salvation. Once a person receives Jesus Christ as their Lord and Savior, at salvation, the Holy Spirit comes in them. He now helps believers live out the Christian walk.

The third experience is the baptism or filling with the Holy Spirit where He now comes upon you. In Acts 1:8, it says "…you will receive power when the Holy Spirit comes upon you" (Acts 1:8). The Holy Spirit empowers a person to do God's will supernaturally. He will help you do things that normally are impossible for you to do on your own. The Bible calls this anointing the gifts of the Holy Spirit, which are found in Romans 12, 1 Corinthians 12 and 1 Peter 4.

If you have never been filled with the Holy Spirit, and you would like to receive this experience, all you must do is pray <u>in faith</u> from your heart believing He will come upon you. Accept this wonderful experience today! You can pray something like this:

Lord Jesus, I ask in faith that Your Holy Spirit supernatural power be poured out upon me. Fill me with Your Holy Spirit. I receive this baptism or filling in faith, in Jesus' name, Amen.

Now believe in your heart that the Holy Spirit filled you today with His anointing power to do His will. Watch over the next 24 hours to see if there is a different motivation in your expression of faith.

You may become a bolder witness or be willing to die for the cause of Christ. You may have a burden to evangelize. Look up Luke 4:18-19. You may even have those desires now in your heart. You may even receive the ability to speak in tongues.

———————◆———————

Mental

———————◆———————

In general, a person's mind consists of positive or negative thoughts. Influenced by what enters the mind and heart through what you listen to, watch, and take part in, will form your actions. Bible says in Philippians 4:8, "…whatever is true, whatever is noble, whatever is right, whatever is pure, whatever is lovely, whatever is admirable—if anything is excellent or praiseworthy—think about such things."

"Do not conform to the pattern of this world but be transformed by the renewing of your mind. Then you will be able to evaluate and approve what God's will is— His good, pleasing, and perfect will" (Romans 12:2).

Start practicing writing down one thing everyday that happened to you that was positive. Look for the positive in every situation. This will help renew your mind in a positive way. Even if it is just something small, like the color of your shoes that brings a smile on your face. You become what you think about all the time, so think positive thoughts.

"Casting down arguments and every high thing that exalts itself against the knowledge of God, bringing every thought into captivity to the obedience of Christ" (2 Corinthians 10:5, NKJV)

Ask for wisdom and strength by the power of the Holy Spirit to take captive every thought that enters your mind. Where we are is a result of how we have been thinking. Do your thoughts align with who you are as a Christ follower? Set your mind on the things above and take control of how you think!

—◆—

Social/Emotional

—◆—

Social skills are a lifetime of learning through wisdom and influence. Cultures have changed and languages along with it. The ability to bring value into your relationship and switch from wrong influences is an art. Understanding the desires of the Lord brings change. The Bible says in Ephesians 4:29, 31-32,

> Do not let any unwholesome talk come out of your mouth, but only what is helpful for building others up according to their needs, that it may help those who listen… Get rid of all bitterness, rage, and anger, brawling, and slander, along with every form of malice. Be kind and compassionate to one another, forgiving each other, just as in Christ, God forgave you.

If you apply this principle alone, it will be effective in your relationships. Without the Lord's presence, you can become hardhearted. Satan can bring a host of unwanted, regretful words and actions into your life. This can offend the very person God wants to reach through you.

Honor and Respect

To have a better social life it is good to treat others with honor and respect. Honor focuses on building up another person's reputation in a positive way. Respect someone by accepting them for who they are even though they are different from you.

- First: Honor and glorify the Lord your God. "Love the Lord your God with all your heart and with all your soul and with all your strength" (Deuteronomy 6:5).

- Second: Honor and support your family. "He must manage his own family well and see that his children obey him with proper respect…If anyone does not provide for his relatives, and especially for his immediate family, he has denied the faith and is worse than an unbeliever" (I Timothy 3:4; 5:8).

- Third: Honor and respect your friends, neighbors, and acquaintances. It may be their divine appointment, as well as yours. "For this reason, make every effort to add to your faith goodness; and to goodness, knowledge; and to knowledge, self-control; and to self-control, perseverance; and to perseverance, godliness; and to godliness, brotherly kindness; and to brotherly kindness, love." (2 Peter 1:5-7).

Your Identity in Jesus Christ

Take the time to look up the following verses listed below. Write down your identity in Christ and begin verbalizing who you are in Christ each day. Example: Romans 3:24 - "...and are justified freely by His grace through the redemption that came by Christ Jesus."

I am justified. (Declared "not guilty" of my sins)

Romans 8:2

_____

I Corinthians 1:2, 30

_____

I Corinthians 15:22

_____

II Corinthians 5:17, 21

_____

Galatians 3:29

_____

Ephesians 1: 3-14

_____

Ephesians 2: 10, 13

_____

Ephesians 3: 6, 12

_____

Ephesians 5: 29-30

_____

Colossians 2: 10-11

_____

Mentors, Friends, and Teachers

Ask the Lord to bring people into your life who can inspire you to grow and mature as a Christian. (*A mentor, one who has experience in the growth you desire; a Christian friend, who is supportive in strengthening weakened areas of your life; or a teacher, who can influence and teach you what you need to know.*)

Make it a priority to seek out those who are encouraging, and the Lord will bring remarkable change into your life through them.

STOP!
Pray to the Lord for someone special (a mentor, friend, or teacher) from whom you would enjoy learning. As a child of God, you can be all that God has designed you to be.

Mentor's name: _____

Learn to mentor.

Making a difference in the lives of those around you brings innumerable rewards for the Kingdom. "Brothers, if someone caught in a sin, you who are spiritual should restore him gently. However, watch yourself, or you also may be tempted. Carry each other's burdens, and in this way, you will fulfill the law of Christ" (Gal. 6:1-2).

"Greater love has no one than this that he lay down his life for his friends" (John 15:13).

"Do not forget to entertain strangers, for by doing so some people have entertained angels without knowing it" (Hebrews 13:2).

Physical

Are you taking care of your body? Staying healthy is essential, and it includes how you rest, the exercise you get, and what you eat to support your body. Whatever you do to your body, you are doing to the Holy Spirit.

> Do you not know that your body is the temple of the Holy Spirit, who is in you, whom you have received from God? You are not your own; you were brought at a price. Therefore, honor God with your body (I Corinthians 6:19-20).

Proper Rest

God gives sleep to regenerate your body so you can take on the daily physical activities. The last few things on your mind affect how you sleep and dream. There are people whose lives have been changed in a positive way by not eating late at night, turning off the phone and not taking phone calls after 8 pm, or watching TV.

The last few hours should be a quiet exit from the day, whether listening to quiet Christian music, singing a favorite hymn, taking an evening walk, reading good literature from respectable authors, picking Bible stories that quiet the mind, or placing yourself in the beauty of what Heaven must be like. Forgive your shortcomings, and always remove negative thoughts about the day.

Try for eight to ten hours of sleep, and then it is time to wake up. First thing in the morning, place yourself before the Father, and let Him guide your day.

Proper Exercise

Depending on your age and ability, a good workout every day is essential. Deep breathing is critical for the mind to have clean fresh air to promote those neurons into sparking. A good sweat releases toxins that have been dormant in your muscles. Toxins cause pain, swelling, and stiffness. Drink water during your exercise to flush your system.

Proper Nutrition

Get informed: Eating fresh food rather than processed is much healthier. A chemical introduced into foods to preserve them is very harmful. If you cannot read it, do not eat it! Sugar intake kills the white blood cell fighting agents you need to keep yourself healthy. If you destroy them, you will suffer untold sicknesses and diseases. Fried foods and salt are your enemies; they can cause clogged arteries, high blood pressure, heart, and kidney disease. Your body is three-quarters water. Denying it prevents your body from recycling your system and purifying harmful acids. The best time to finish your last meal of the day is no later than 7:00 pm. Your digestive system is designed to slow down as you rest from your daily activities. Principle Solution: Eat breakfast like a King, lunch like a Prince, and dinner like a pauper.

Financial

Budgeting is a plan that saves families from financial disasters. Areas to consider are giving, saving, and spending. God calls us to manage the resources He has given us with good stewardship.

The Bible speaks of God's care for the weak, poor, and needy, and His blessing on those who share this concern. God wants our generosity to reflect His own free giving. As He has blessed us, we should also bless others.

Psalm 112:5 says, "Good will come to him who is generous and lends freely..." Generosity should cure two problems that money can create:

1) The rich man may abuse others in his desire to accumulate wealth. Generosity will end the abuse. 2) The fear of losing money can be a snare. Generosity and respect for God places our trust and security in Him, not our money.

II Corinthians 9:7 says, "Each man should give what he has decided in his heart to give not reluctantly or under compulsion, for God loves a cheerful giver." Our attitude when we give is more important than the amount we give.

Proverbs 19:17 says, "He who is kind to the poor lends to the Lord, and He will reward him for what he has done." Here God identifies with the poor as Jesus does in Matthew 25:31-46.

According to the NIV *Life Application Bible* commentary (1991): "God will separate His obedient followers from the pretenders and unbelievers. The real evidence of our belief is the way we act. Treat all people we meet as if they are Jesus is not easy. What we do for others shows what we really think about Jesus' words to us—feed the hungry, give a place to stay to homeless, look after the sick.

How well do your actions separate you from the pretenders and unbelievers? We have no excuse to neglect those who have deep needs, and we cannot hand over this responsibility to the church or government. Jesus demands our personal involvement in caring for other's needs. God wants our service to go beyond our own personal growth to acts of kindness, charity, justice, and generosity."

The Bible says in Proverbs 28: 27, "He who gives to the poor will not lack..."

There are four key principles of giving in II Cor. 8:10-15 (from NIV *Life Application Bible* (1991) commentary):

> 1) Give with a cheerful heart no matter how small.
> 2) Meet the needs of others.
> 3) Give without expecting anything in return.
> 4) Strive to fulfill any financial commitment.

God will supply all our needs, and He usually does this through other people.

What can you do today to help God supply someone's needs? Do it!

Tithing Is Important

Tithing is giving back to the Lord what He has given you. The Bible says in Proverbs 3:9, "Honor the Lord with your wealth..." You may not understand what tithing means. Tithing is giving the first fruits to the Lord! The first fruits consist of money, time, possessions, and talent. Show the Lord how much you love Him by giving back to Him that which He has given you. Your understanding and maturity reflect your giving. It shows how much you truly love God. Malachi 3:10 says:

Bring the whole tithe in the storehouse, that there may be food in My house. 'Test Me in this,' says the Lord Almighty, 'and see if I will not throw open the floodgates of heaven and pour out so much blessing that you will not have room enough for it.

Solutions to Indebtedness

Below is a list of ways you can set a budget and save money. This can work if applied.

- Remove unnecessary expenses that are eating away at your income.
- Cease using credit cards, unless disciplined to pay off monthly. Credit cards can produce impulse buying.
- Minimize eating out and junk food. It is costly.
- Avoid gimmicks and gadgets that either fall apart or become cluttered with no function.
- Skip the lotto, gambling, or money schemes, i.e., "get rich quick" businesses.

Plan for Emergencies

If you have never saved money before, start setting aside just a little bit from your paycheck every time paid. This will add up quicker than you expect. A good goal is 10% of your income but start with something. Do it faithfully and you will reach your desired emergency fund. An emergency fund is not for a new T.V., couch. It is for truly necessary unexpected problems, i.e., car repair, medical care, and urgent household repairs. Tithing and saving for emergencies will bring you more peace of mind with your finances.

It is important to write out your goals and review them on a regular basis. This will make you more accountable to follow through with God's plans for your life. Find activities that will allow you to use the gifts and talents that God has given you.

- What are your unique gifts and talents?

  _____

  _____

  _____

- What are your passions or desires?

  _____

  _____

  _____

- What type of legacy do you want to leave behind?

  _____

  _____

  _____

From what you've learned on the five life disciplines, make specific goals for your life.

Each week you will have an opportunity to set smaller goals to reach your life goals or help bring growth and refinement. These smaller goals may be the same throughout the study to better reinforce them.

Let God lead you in setting your goals.

Questions to ask God when setting your goals:

- Do I need this? Will this help me?
- Does it help others see Christ in me?
- Will I become stronger in Christ because of it?

Example of Short-Term Goals

Goals	Spiritual	Mental	Social/Emotional	Physical	Financial
New Habit (What…be specific)	Pray in the morning	Read Bible	Say, "Hi!" to a new person	Take a walk	Instead of impulse shopping, Save it.
Measurable Growth (How much … and/or when)	5-10 minutes	15-20 minutes	1-2 new people	15-20 minutes	Give to help others in need
Period (daily, weekly, monthly)	Daily	Daily	Weekly	Daily	Monthly

Your Life Goals and Refining Goals

Spiritual

Life Goals:

1. _____
2. _____
3. _____

Refining Goals: *Where is <u>God leading</u> you to bring growth and refinement into your life?*

1. Meditate on Scripture & Pray daily.
2. Attend church weekly & Write down what God is doing in your life.
3. Serve in a ministry or go on a mission's trip.

Mental

Life Goals:

1. _____
2. _____
3. _____

Refining Goals: *Where is <u>God leading</u> you to bring growth and refinement into your life?*

1. God, what should I be thinking?

   _____

2. God, what should I be reading & watching?

   _____

3. God, what should I be hearing & saying?

   _____

Social/Emotional

Life Goals:

1. _____
2. _____
3. _____

Refining Goals: *Where is* <u>*God leading*</u> *you to bring growth and refinement into your life?*

1. Choose wisely your mentors/coaches/teachers/friends/social involvements.
2. Relate to your family in a godly way.
3. Treat others with (love, patience, kindness, gentleness, compassion, forgiveness, and respect)

Physical

Life Goals:

1. _____
2. _____
3. _____

Refining Goals: *Where is* <u>*God leading*</u> *you to bring growth and refinement into your life?*

1. Exercise ideas: walking, running, biking, hiking, aerobics, water aerobics, playing sports, skiing, weightlifting, swimming, jump roping, tennis.
2. Eat or drink more _____ and less of _____
3. Stop and seek help with any addiction issues.

Financial

Life Goals:

1. _____
2. _____
3. _____

Refining Goals: *Where is* <u>*God leading*</u> *you to bring growth and refinement into your life?*

1. Tithe (_____ %) & Give more generously to others.
2. Pay toward debt _____
3. Budget & Save about $1000 – $10,000 in an emergency fund.

STOP!
Take time to fill out your Short-Term Goals, Life Goals and Refining Goals.

Develop the new habit over time. It usually takes twenty-one days before a habit reaches your subconscious and can start becoming automatic. So be patient in the process and never give up!

Short-Term Goals

Goals	Spiritual	Mental	Social/Emotional	Physical	Financial
New Habit (What...be specific)					
Measurable Growth (How much ... and/or when)					
Period (daily, weekly, monthly)					

Notes & Reflections

_____
_____
_____
_____
_____
_____
_____
_____
_____
_____
_____
_____
_____
_____

Praise

Repent

Ask

Yield

Week One

Beginning Your Journey

---◆---

Now that each of the five disciplines have been explained, it is time to start doing the daily bible time of journaling with the Lord about what you are learning and to sit quietly with Him to allow Him to speak to you personally in His still small voice. Look up 1 Kings 19:9-18 to learn about this still small voice.

Before beginning each lesson for the day, PRAY!

Example prayer: *Lord, open my eyes that I may see wonderful things in Your Word. Allow the Holy Spirit to guide me into all truth and tell me what is yet to come. May the Holy Spirit bring glory to You by taking from what is Yours and making it known and alive for me! Reveal to me who You are, Your truth, power, and what knowledge of You and Your Word that You want me to gain and know. In Jesus' Name, Amen.*

Weekly Lessons
Each lesson will consist of:
- Choosing a life goal or growth and refinement goal to focus on each day.
- Reading the Scripture passage. Allow the Scriptures to come alive for you. The Holy Spirit will teach you through God's Word everything you need to know. Meditate on what He is teaching you.
- Writing out your responses to the questions and the memory verse for the week from the Bible version you choose to use throughout the study.
- Sit before the Lord to see what He has to say to you. At the end of the day, reflect on what God may have done and write out any prayer requests you received during the day.

Church Notes/Review
Begin developing a habit of taking sermon notes from your church services. This will help you remember what God is speaking into your life and how you need to apply it. You will also have the chance to review and remember each week's highlights and most meaningful lessons.

Goals	Spiritual	Mental	Social/ Emotional	Physical	Financial
New Habit (What…be specific)					
Measurable Growth (How much and/or when)					
Period (daily, weekly, monthly)					

Week One

Day: _____ Date: _____ Time: _____

Scripture Reading: Gospel of John 1:1-18

What did you learn from today's reading, and how does it apply to your life?

_____

_____

_____

_____

_____

What characteristics from the passage do you want to display in your life?

_____

_____

_____

_____

What specific goal have you set for your Spiritual growth and refinement for this week? What is your progress?

_____

_____

Write out your memory verse for this week: *Romans 10:9-10, 13.*

_____

_____

_____

_____

_____

_____

Write three things you are grateful for today.

_____

_____

_____

Write out a prayer to God in response to what you have learned in today's lesson.

_____

_____

_____

_____

_____

Ask, "Lord, what do You want to say to me personally about grace and truth?"

_____

_____

_____

_____

_____

Reflection: Did you experience God in a special way today or yesterday? How?

_____

_____

_____

_____

Additional Note Space is provided at the end of each week & at the back of the book for prayers, journaling, etc.

Pray for: Someone to be saved _____ someone to disciple _____

Date	Prayer Requests Received Today	How and when answered? (Come back and follow up as needed)

Week One

Day: _____ Date: _____ Time: _____

Lesson 2: John the Baptist

Scripture Reading: Gospel of John 1:19-28

What did you learn in today's reading? How will you apply it to your life?

_____

_____

_____

_____

Have you been water baptized? If so, share your experience. If not, why not?

_____

_____

_____

_____

_____

_____

What specific goal have you set for your Mental growth and refinement this week? What is your progress?

_____

_____

Write out your memory verse for this week: *Romans 10:9-10, 13.*

_____

_____

_____

_____

_____

Write three things you are grateful for today.

_____

_____

_____

Write out a prayer to God in response to what you have learned in today's lesson.

_____

_____

_____

_____

_____

_____

Ask, "Lord, what do You want to say to me personally about pride and humility?"

_____

_____

_____

_____

_____

_____

Reflection: Did you experience God in a special way today or yesterday? How?

_____

_____

_____

_____

_____

Pray for: Someone to be saved _____ someone to disciple _____

Date	Prayer Requests Received Today	How and when answered? (Come back and follow up as needed)

Week One

Day: _____ Date: _____ Time: _____

Lesson 3: Lamb of God

Scripture Reading: Gospel of John 1:29-34

What did you learn in today's reading? How will you apply it to your life?

_____

_____

_____

_____

Have you been filled with the Holy Spirit? If so, share your experience. If not, why not?

_____

_____

_____

_____

_____

_____

What specific goal have you set for your Social/Emotional growth and refinement for this week? What is your progress?

_____

_____

Write the memory verse for this week: *Romans 10:9-10, 13.*

_____

_____

_____

_____

_____

Write out three things you are grateful for in your life today.

_____

_____

_____

Write out a prayer to God in response to what you have learned in today's lesson.

_____

_____

_____

_____

_____

Ask, "Lord, what do You want to say to me personally about teaching the message of repentance and salvation?"

_____

_____

_____

_____

_____

Reflection: How did you experience God in a special way today or yesterday?

_____

_____

_____

_____

_____

Pray for: Someone to be saved _____ someone to disciple _____

Date	Prayer Requests Received Today	How and when answered? (Come back and follow up as needed)

Week One

Lesson 4: First Disciples

Scripture Reading: Gospel of John 1:35-42

What did you learn in today's reading? How will you apply it to your life?

_____

_____

_____

_____

Who can you bring to see Jesus? And are you personally taking time to follow Jesus? How?

_____

_____

_____

_____

_____

_____

What specific goal have you set for your Physical growth and refinement for this week? What is your progress?

_____

_____

Write the memory verse for this week: *Romans 10:9-10, 13.*

_____

_____

_____

_____

_____

_____

Write three things you can be grateful for today.

_____

_____

_____

Write your prayer to God responding to what you learned in today's Scriptures.

_____

_____

_____

_____

_____

_____

Ask, "Lord, what do You want to say to me personally about following Jesus?"

_____

_____

_____

_____

_____

_____

Reflection: How did you experience God in a special way today or yesterday?

_____

_____

_____

_____

Pray for: Someone to be saved _____ someone to disciple _____

Date	Prayer Requests Received Today	How and when answered? (Come back and follow up as needed)

Week One

Day: _____ Date: _____ Time: _____

Scripture Reading: Gospel of John 1:43-51

What did you learn in today's reading? How will you apply it to your life?

_____

_____

_____

_____

_____

After meditating on this passage, what word(s), or phrases came alive and spoke to your heart?

_____

_____

_____

_____

_____

What specific goal have you set for your Financial growth and refinement for this week? What is your progress?

_____

_____

Write the memory verse for this week: *Romans 10:9-10, 13.*

_____

_____

_____

_____

_____

_____

Write out three things you are grateful for today.

_____

_____

_____

Write out a prayer to God in response to what you learned in this lesson.

_____

_____

_____

_____

_____

Ask, "Lord, what do You want to say to me personally about how You see me?"

_____

_____

_____

_____

_____

Reflection: How did you experience God in a special way today or yesterday?

_____

_____

_____

_____

_____

Pray for: Someone to be saved _____ someone to disciple _____

Date	Prayer Requests Received Today	How and when answered? (Come back and follow up as needed)

Notes

$\mathcal{B}$egin each day with
prayer; wait on the Lord.

"Seek first the kingdom of
God and His
righteousness and all
these things will be added
to you."
– Matthew 6:33 ESV

Church Sermon Notes

———◆———

Theme:

_____

_____

_____

Scriptures:

_____

_____

_____

Lessons:

_____

_____

_____

_____

_____

Application:

_____

_____

_____

_____

_____

Notes:

_____

_____

_____

_____

_____

Things to Remember from Week One

———————◆———————

Scriptures:

_____

_____

_____

Application:

_____

_____

_____

Goals Set:

_____

_____

_____

Memory Verse:

_____

_____

_____

Time with God:

_____

_____

_____

Reflection:

_____

_____

_____

Answered Prayers:

_____

_____

_____

Week Two

Obedience

———◆———

Obedience is of utmost importance for every Christian. Following through on your goals will help you see growth take place as you obey what God is revealing to you. **Change is inevitable – Growth is a choice. For every decision you make today, there is a choice that is pleasing to God** (Anonymous).

Keep your Life Goals and Refining Goals in front of you. This will help you stay focused and keep you accountable. By keeping track of your progress, it will help you set up new habits, see measurable growth, and it will all be done within a specific period. Frequent evaluation of these goals can help you press on to reach the goals set before you.

When setting your goals, ask yourself: Do I need this, will this help me, and does it bring glory to God? Write out your goals from last week to keep them in mind until the new habit is formed. Make any needed adjustments.

Goals	Spiritual	Mental	Social/ Emotional	Physical	Financial
New Habit (What…be specific)					
Measurable Growth (How much and/or when)					
Period (daily, weekly, monthly)					

Week Two

Day: _____ Date: _____ Time: _____

Lesson 1: The Word of Life

Scripture Reading: I John 1:1-4

What did you learn in today's reading? How will you apply it to your life?

_____

_____

_____

_____

_____

_____

Based on your study of this passage, what does it mean to have fellowship with God and with each other? How can you encourage greater fellowship?

_____

_____

_____

_____

_____

What specific goal have you set for your Spiritual growth and refinement for this week? What is your progress?

_____

_____

_____

Write the memory verse for this week: *Acts 1:8.*

_____

_____

_____

Write three things you are grateful for today.

_____

_____

_____

Write out a prayer to God responding to today's lesson.

_____

_____

_____

_____

_____

Ask, "Lord, what do You want to say to me personally about sharing the testimony of Jesus Christ?"

_____

_____

_____

_____

_____

Reflection: How did you experience God in a special way today or yesterday?

_____

_____

_____

_____

_____

Pray for: Someone to be saved _____ someone to disciple _____

Date	Prayer Requests Received Today	How and when answered? (Come back and follow up as needed)

Week Two

Lesson 2: Walking in the Light

Scripture Reading: I John 1:5-2:2.

What did you learn in today's reading? How will you apply it to your life?

_____

_____

_____

_____

_____

_____

Hearing the voice of God only matters when you obey the voice of God, so who do you need to forgive? Write out a statement of forgiveness as needed.

_____

_____

_____

_____

_____

What specific goal have you set for your Mental growth and refinement for this week? What is your progress?

_____

_____

Write the memory verse for this week: *Acts 1:8.*

_____

_____

_____

Write three things you are grateful for today.

_____

_____

_____

Write out a prayer to God responding to today's lesson.

_____

_____

_____

_____

_____

_____

Ask, "Lord, reveal to me any sins that I need to confess so that I can be forgiven and purified."

_____

_____

_____

_____

_____

_____

Reflection: How did you experience God in a special way today or yesterday?

_____

_____

_____

_____

Pray for: Someone to be saved _____ someone to disciple _____

Date	Prayer Requests Received Today	How and when answered? (Come back and follow up as needed)

Week Two

Day: _____ Date: _____ Time: _____

Scripture Reading: I John 2:3-11

What did you learn in today's reading? How will you apply it to your life?

_____

_____

_____

_____

_____

_____

After reading that obedience to God illustrates our love for one another, what must change in your life, so you are displaying more of His love?

_____

_____

_____

_____

_____

_____

_____

What specific goal have you set for your Social/Emotional growth and refinement this week? What is your progress?

_____

_____

Write the memory verse for this week: *Acts 1:8.*

_____

_____

_____

Write out three things you are grateful for today.

_____

_____

_____

Write out a prayer to God responding to today's lesson.

_____

_____

_____

_____

_____

_____

Ask, "Lord, reveal to me anyone that I have hatred toward or need to forgive and why?"

_____

_____

_____

_____

_____

_____

Reflection: How did you experience God in a special way today or yesterday?

_____

_____

_____

_____

Pray for: Someone to be saved _____ someone to disciple _____

Date	Prayer Requests Received Today	How and when answered? (Come back and follow up as needed)

Week Two

Day: _____ Date: _____ Time: _____

Lesson 4: Spiritual State

Scripture Reading: I John 2:12-14

What did you learn in today's reading? How will you apply it to your life?

_____

_____

_____

_____

_____

_____

How can you overcome the evil one?

_____

_____

_____

_____

_____

_____

What specific goal have you set for your Physical growth and refinement for this week? What is your progress?

_____

_____

Write the memory verse for this week: *Acts 1:8.*

_____

_____

_____

Write out three things you are grateful for today.

_____

_____

_____

Write out a prayer to God responding to today's lesson.

_____

_____

_____

_____

_____

_____

Ask, "Lord, what do You want to say to me personally about overcoming the evil one?"

_____

_____

_____

_____

_____

Reflection: How did you experience God in a special way today or yesterday?

_____

_____

_____

_____

Pray for: Someone to be saved _____ someone to disciple _____

Date	Prayer Requests Received Today	How and when answered? (Come back and follow up as needed)

Week Two

Lesson 5: Do Not Love the World

Scripture Reading: I John 2:15-17

What did you learn in today's reading? How will you apply it to your life?

_____

_____

_____

_____

_____

_____

After meditating on this passage, how will you separate from worldly things?

_____

_____

_____

_____

_____

_____

What specific goal have you set for your Financial growth and refinement for this week? What is your progress?

_____

_____

_____

Write the memory verse for this week: *Acts 1:8.*

_____

_____

_____

Write out three things you are grateful for today.

_____

_____

_____

Write out a prayer to God responding to today's lesson.

_____

_____

_____

_____

_____

Ask, "Lord, what do You want to say to me personally about cravings, lust, and boasting?"

_____

_____

_____

_____

_____

Reflection: How did you experience God in a special way today or yesterday?

_____

_____

_____

_____

Pray for: Someone to be saved _____ someone to disciple _____

Date	Prayer Requests Received Today	How and when answered? (Come back and follow up as needed)

Notes

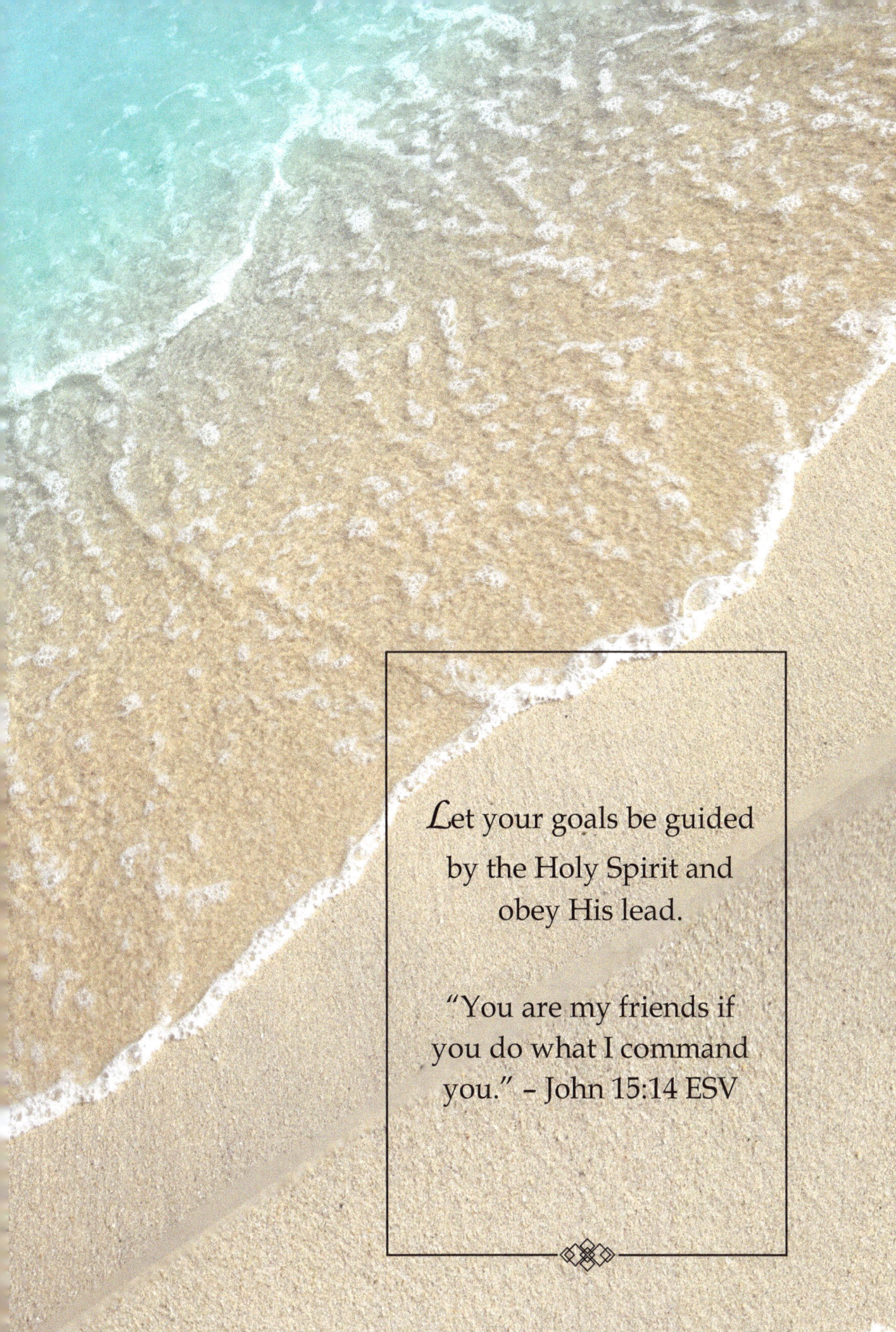

$\mathcal{L}$et your goals be guided
by the Holy Spirit and
obey His lead.

"You are my friends if
you do what I command
you." – John 15:14 ESV

Church Sermon Notes

———◆———

Theme:

_____

_____

_____

Scriptures:

_____

_____

_____

Lessons:

_____

_____

_____

_____

_____

_____

Application:

_____

_____

_____

_____

_____

_____

Notes:

_____

_____

_____

_____

_____

Things to Remember from Week Two

Scriptures:

_____

_____

_____

Application:

_____

_____

_____

Goals Set:

_____

_____

_____

Memory Verse:

_____

_____

_____

Time with God:

_____

_____

_____

Reflection:

_____

_____

_____

Answered Prayers:

_____

_____

_____

Week Three

Scripture Memorization

———————◆———————

By memorizing Scripture, you will be putting God's Word in your heart and mind. Key ways to memorize Scripture:

- Write the Scripture out on an index card and carry it with you.
- Speak it aloud using the reference before and after the verse.
- Repeat small phrases at a time.
- Discover the meaning of the Scripture verse.
- Visualize it as you say it.
- Place your name in the Scripture verse to make it personal.
- Record yourself saying it and then listen to it repeatedly.

Be sure you are journaling what God is doing in your life, so you can look back and praise Him for what He has done, is doing, and will do in your life. What changes have you noticed in your life from doing this study? How has God spoken to your heart?

Write out your goals from last week to keep them in mind until the new habit is formed. Make any needed adjustments.

Goals	Spiritual	Mental	Social/ Emotional	Physical	Financial
New Habit (What…be specific)					
Measurable Growth (How much and/or when)					
Period (daily, weekly, monthly)					

Week Three

Day: _____ Date: _____ Time: _____

Scripture Reading: I John 2:18-27

What did you learn in today's reading? How will you apply it to your life?

_____

_____

_____

_____

_____

What must change in your life to continue in sound doctrine of submission to the Spirit and the practice of righteousness? What is your main reason for being a Christian?

_____

_____

_____

_____

_____

_____

What specific goal have you set for your Spiritual growth and refinement for this week? What is your progress?

_____

_____

Write the memory verse for this week: *Joshua 1:8.*

_____

_____

_____

_____

Write out three things you are grateful for today.

_____

_____

_____

Write out a prayer to God responding to today's lesson.

_____

_____

_____

_____

_____

_____

Ask, "Lord, what do You want to say to me personally about the anointing that You have placed on me?"

_____

_____

_____

_____

_____

_____

Reflection: How did you experience God in a special way today or yesterday?

_____

_____

_____

_____

Pray for: Someone to be saved _____ someone to disciple _____

Date	Prayer Requests Received Today	How and when answered? (Come back and follow up as needed)

Week Three

Day: _____ Date: _____ Time: _____

Scripture Reading: I John 2:28 – 3:3.

What did you learn in today's reading? How will you apply it to your life?

_____

_____

_____

_____

_____

After realizing that a Christian's life is not characterized by sin, what must change in your life so that you are living as God wants?

_____

_____

_____

_____

_____

What specific goal have you set for your Mental growth and refinement for this week? What is your progress?

_____

_____

Write the memory verse for this week: *Joshua 1:8.*

_____

_____

_____

_____

Write out three things you are grateful for today.

_____

_____

_____

Write out a prayer to God responding to today's lesson.

_____

_____

_____

_____

_____

_____

Ask, "Lord, what do You want to say to me personally about being confident and unashamed before You?"

_____

_____

_____

_____

_____

_____

Reflection: How did you experience God in a special way today or yesterday?

_____

_____

_____

_____

Pray for: Someone to be saved _____ someone to disciple _____

Date	Prayer Requests Received Today	How and when answered? (Come back and follow up as needed)

Week Three

Day: _____ Date: _____ Time: _____

Lesson 3: Sin and Lawlessness

Scripture Reading: I John 3:4-10

What did you learn in today's reading? How will you apply it to your life?

_____

_____

_____

_____

_____

What sinful deliberate habits do you need to confess before God as incompatible with your holy calling?

_____

_____

_____

_____

_____

_____

What specific goal have you set for your Social/Emotional growth and refinement for this week? What is your progress?

_____

_____

Write the memory verse for this week: *Joshua 1:8.*

_____

_____

_____

_____

Write out three things you are grateful for today.

_____

_____

_____

Write a prayer to God responding to today's lesson.

_____

_____

_____

_____

_____

_____

Ask, "Lord, what do You want to say to me personally about my walk with You and how I live my life?"

_____

_____

_____

_____

_____

_____

Reflection: How did you experience God in a special way today or yesterday?

_____

_____

_____

_____

Pray for: Someone to be saved _____ someone to disciple _____

Date	Prayer Requests Received Today	How and when answered? (Come back and follow up as needed)

Week Three

Day: _____ Date: _____ Time: _____

Lesson 4: Urgency of Love

Scripture Reading: I John 3:11-15

What did you learn in today's reading? How will you apply it to your life?

_____

_____

_____

_____

_____

What does a life of moral purity look like? How will you live it out?

_____

_____

_____

_____

_____

What specific goal have you set for your Physical growth and refinement for this week? What is your progress?

_____

_____

Write the memory verse for this week: *Joshua 1:8.*

_____

_____

_____

_____

_____

Write out three things you are grateful for today.

_____

_____

_____

Write out a prayer to God responding to today's lesson.

_____

_____

_____

_____

_____

_____

Ask, "Lord, what do You want to say to me personally about my relationships with others?"

_____

_____

_____

_____

_____

_____

Reflection: How did you experience God in a special way today or yesterday?

_____

_____

_____

_____

Pray for: Someone to be saved _____ someone to disciple _____

Date	Prayer Requests Received Today	How and when answered? (Come back and follow up as needed)

Week Three

Day: _____ Date: _____ Time: _____

Scripture Reading: I John 3:16-24

What did you learn in today's reading? How will you apply it to your life?

_____

_____

_____

_____

_____

We must obey the command to believe in the name of Jesus Christ and love one another, what must change in your life, so you are loving others as God wants? How will you live it out?

_____

_____

_____

_____

_____

_____

What specific goal have you set for your Financial growth and refinement for this week? What is your progress?

_____

_____

Write the memory verse for this week: *Joshua 1:8.*

_____

_____

_____

_____

Write out three things you are grateful for today.

_____

_____

_____

Write out a prayer to God responding to today's lesson.

_____

_____

_____

_____

_____

_____

Ask, "Lord, what do You want to say to me personally about laying down my life for others?"

_____

_____

_____

_____

_____

Reflection: How did you experience God in a special way today or yesterday?

_____

_____

_____

_____

Pray for: Someone to be saved _____ someone to disciple _____

Date	Prayer Requests Received Today	How and when answered? (Come back and follow up as needed)

Notes

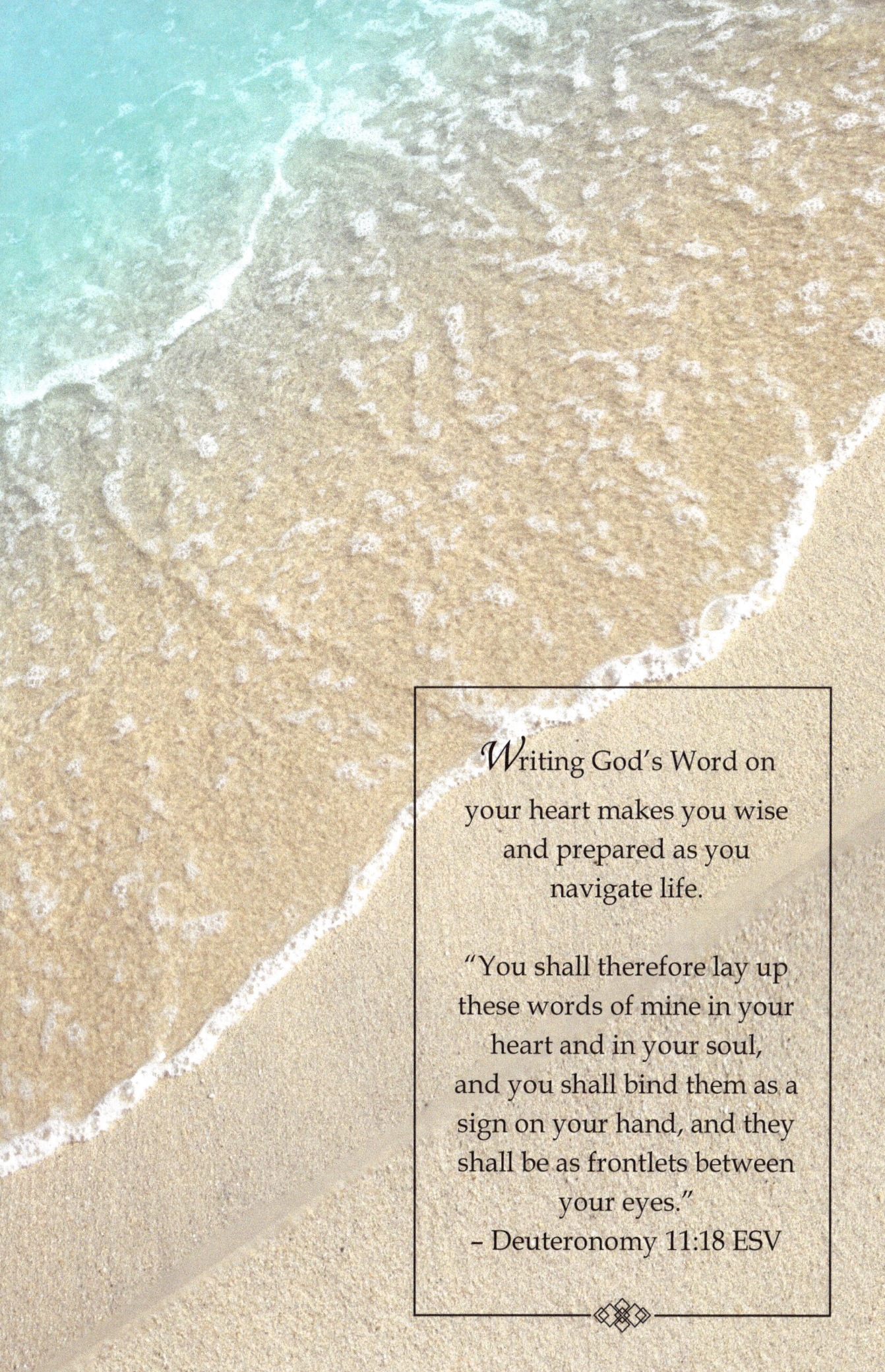

*W*riting God's Word on your heart makes you wise and prepared as you navigate life.

"You shall therefore lay up these words of mine in your heart and in your soul, and you shall bind them as a sign on your hand, and they shall be as frontlets between your eyes."
– Deuteronomy 11:18 ESV

Church Sermon Notes

———————◆———————

Theme:

_____

_____

_____

Scriptures:

_____

_____

_____

Lessons:

_____

_____

_____

_____

_____

_____

Application:

_____

_____

_____

_____

_____

_____

Notes:

_____

_____

_____

_____

_____

Church Sermon Notes

———◆———

Theme:

_____

_____

_____

Scriptures:

_____

_____

_____

Lessons:

_____

_____

_____

_____

_____

_____

Application:

_____

_____

_____

_____

_____

_____

Notes:

_____

_____

_____

_____

_____

Things to Remember from Week Three

———◆———

Scriptures:

_____

_____

_____

Application:

_____

_____

_____

Goals Set:

_____

_____

_____

Memory Verse:

_____

_____

_____

Time with God:

_____

_____

_____

Reflection:

_____

_____

_____

Answered Prayers:

_____

_____

_____

Week Four

Freedom from the Past

During this week, God may set you free from past hurts and challenges. Allow the Truth of God's Word to speak to your heart and consciousness. Our hurt is from our social interactions. A "bitter root" comes when we allow disappointment to grow into resentment, or when we nurse a grudge over past hurts. To heal, you must forgive the person, their actions, or the words said to you. If you do not forgive them, you will never really be free from the spirit of bitterness, which is a stronghold.

Mathias (2010) said in his book, *Biblical Foundations of Freedom*, "Bitterness enters first through unforgiveness, then through resentment, retaliation, anger, hatred, violence, and even murder" (p.75). If not dealt with, unforgiveness can lead to violence. The bible says in Hebrews 12:15, "See to it that no one misses the grace of God and that no bitter root grows up to cause trouble and defile many."

Like a small root that grows into a great tree, bitterness springs up in our hearts and overshadows even our deepest Christian relationships. When the Holy Spirit fills us, however, He can heal the hurt that causes bitterness. II Cor. 10:4 says, "The weapons we fight with are not the weapons of the world. On the contrary, they have divine power to demolish strongholds."

God's mighty weapons are prayer, faith, hope, love, His Word, and the Holy Spirit, which are all powerful and effective. These weapons break down the walls Satan builds. *Nothing* can break down these barriers like God's weapons.

This week, see if you hear or read repetitive Scripture verses in different circumstances of your life. What are these verses saying to you?

It could be something that God wants you to change. Accept this change with perseverance. Share any struggles you may be having with your accountability partner so they can pray for you.

Goals	Spiritual	Mental	Social/ Emotional	Physical	Financial
New Habit (What…be specific)					
Measurable Growth (How much and/or when)					
Period (daily, weekly, monthly)					

Week Four

Day: _____ Date: _____Time: _____

Lesson 1: The New Birth

Scripture Reading: Gospel of John 3:1-21

What did you learn in today's reading? How will you apply it to your life?

_____

_____

_____

_____

_____

_____

Have you been born again? If so, share your experience. If not, why not?

_____

_____

_____

_____

_____

_____

_____

_____

_____

What specific goal have you set for your Spiritual growth and refinement this week? What is your progress?

_____

_____

Write the memory verse for this week: *I John 1:9.*

_____

_____

_____

Write out three things you are grateful for today.

_____

_____

_____

Write out a prayer to God responding to today's lesson.

_____

_____

_____

_____

_____

_____

Ask, "Lord, what do You want to say to me personally about my new birth?"

_____

_____

_____

_____

_____

_____

Reflection: How did you experience God in a special way today or yesterday?

_____

_____

_____

_____

Pray for: Someone to be saved _____ someone to disciple _____

Date	Prayer Requests Received Today	How and when answered? (Come back and follow up as needed)

Week Four

Day: _____ Date: _____ Time: _____

Scripture Reading: I John 4:1-6

What did you learn in today's reading? How will you apply it to your life?

_____

_____

_____

_____

_____

_____

How can you evaluate the spirits to know if they are of God or not?

_____

_____

_____

_____

_____

_____

What specific goal have you set for your Mental growth and refinement for this week? What is your progress?

_____

_____

Write the memory verse for this week: *I John 1:9.*

_____

_____

_____

Write out three things you are grateful for today.

_____

_____

_____

Write out a prayer to God responding to today's lesson.

_____

_____

_____

_____

_____

_____

Ask, "Lord, what do You want to say to me personally about how I am acknowledging who Jesus is?"

_____

_____

_____

_____

_____

_____

Reflection: How did you experience God in a special way today or yesterday?

_____

_____

_____

_____

Pray for: Someone to be saved _____ someone to disciple _____

Date	Prayer Requests Received Today	How and when answered? (Come back and follow up as needed)

Week Four

Day: _____ Date: _____ Time: _____

Scripture Reading: I John 4:7-11

What did you learn in today's reading? How will you apply it to your life?

_____

_____

_____

_____

_____

_____

How do you show love for God in your choices and actions?

_____

_____

_____

_____

_____

_____

What specific goal have you set for your Social/Emotional growth and resentment for this week? What is your progress?

_____

_____

Write the memory verse for this week: *I John 1:9.*

_____

_____

_____

Write out three things you are grateful for today.

_____

_____

_____

Write out a prayer to God responding to today's lesson.

_____

_____

_____

_____

_____

_____

Ask, "Lord, what do You want to say to me personally about how I am showing Your love to others?"

_____

_____

_____

_____

_____

Reflection: How did you experience God in a special way today or yesterday?

_____

_____

_____

_____

Pray for: Someone to be saved _____ someone to disciple _____

Date	Prayer Requests Received Today	How and when answered? (Come back and follow up as needed)

Week Four

Day: _____ Date: _____ Time: _____

Lesson 4: God is Love

Scripture Reading: I John 4:12-17

What did you learn in today's reading? How will you apply it to your life?

_____

_____

_____

_____

_____

_____

Does the love of God live in you? How will or do you live it out?

_____

_____

_____

_____

_____

_____

What specific goal have you set for your Physical growth and refinement for this week? What is your progress?

_____

_____

Write the memory verse for this week: *I John 1:9.*

_____

_____

_____

Write out three things you are grateful for today:

_____

_____

_____

Write out a prayer to God responding to today's lesson.

_____

_____

_____

_____

_____

_____

Ask, "Lord, what do You want to say to me personally about my love toward You and others?"

_____

_____

_____

_____

_____

Reflection: How did you experience God in a special way today or yesterday?

_____

_____

_____

_____

Pray for: Someone to be saved _____ someone to disciple _____

Date	Prayer Requests Received Today	How and when answered? (Come back and follow up as needed)

Week Four

Day: _____ Date: _____ Time: _____

Scripture Reading: I John 4:18-21

What did you learn in today's reading? How will you apply it to your life?

_____

_____

_____

_____

_____

_____

Do you fear anything? If so, what? How can or will you overcome this fear?

_____

_____

_____

_____

_____

_____

What specific goal have you set for your Financial growth and refinement for this week? What is your progress?

_____

_____

Write the memory verse for this week: *I John 1:9.*

_____

_____

_____

Write out three things you are grateful for today:

_____

_____

_____

Write out a prayer to God responding to today's lesson.

_____

_____

_____

_____

_____

Ask, "Lord, what do You want to say to me personally about how to let go of any fear that I have within me?"

_____

_____

_____

_____

_____

Reflection: How did you experience God in a special way today or yesterday?

_____

_____

_____

_____

Pray for: Someone to be saved _____ someone to disciple _____

Date	Prayer Requests Received Today	How and when answered? (Come back and follow up as needed)

Notes

Choose to forgive as you
have been forgiven. Through
forgiveness is great healing
and freedom.

"He forgives all my sins and
heals all my diseases."
– Psalm 103:3 NLT

"Be kind and compassionate
to one another, forgiving
each other, just as in Christ
God forgave you."
– Ephesians 4:32 NIV

Church Sermon Notes

Theme:

_____

_____

_____

Scriptures:

_____

_____

_____

Lessons:

_____

_____

_____

_____

_____

Application:

_____

_____

_____

_____

_____

Notes:

_____

_____

_____

_____

_____

Things to Remember from Week Four

Scriptures:

_____

_____

_____

Application:

_____

_____

_____

Goals Set:

_____

_____

_____

Memory Verse:

_____

_____

_____

Time with God:

_____

_____

_____

Reflection:

_____

_____

_____

Answered Prayers:

_____

_____

_____

Week Five

Affirmations

———•◆•———

As a Christian, God has placed in each believer spiritual gifts. The choices you make can affect whether you manage your spiritual gifts positively or negatively. What you behold, you become. In Romans 12, I Corinthians 12, and 1 Peter 4, the Bible lists the different spiritual gifts.

STOP!
Take time to read about these gifts. Ask God to reveal to you the gift(s) He has placed within you. Then make it a priority to use them to advance the Kingdom of God.

My Spiritual Gifts are....

_____

_____

This week write down affirmations based on the promises of God in Scripture that you will start to walk in. Reference back to what you learned about Identity in Christ on page 25. Start saying them aloud daily. Share your affirmations with your accountability partner to ensure they are positive things that you are saying to yourself, and to hear you say them with passion. I am … I can… I will…

(Example: I am a child of the Most High God, I can do all things through Christ who strengthens me, and I will overcome by the power of the Holy Spirit.)

I am…_____

I can… _____

I will…_____

Goals	Spiritual	Mental	Social/ Emotional	Physical	Financial
New Habit (What…be specific)					
Measurable Growth (How much and/or when)					
Period (daily, weekly, monthly)					

Week Five

Day: _____ Date: _____ Time: _____

Scripture Reading: I John 5:1-5

What did you learn in today's reading? How will you apply it to your life?

_____

_____

_____

_____

_____

Is there any command of God that you are not living out? Why? How will you live it out?

_____

_____

_____

_____

_____

What specific goal have you set for your Spiritual growth and refinement for this week? What is your progress?

_____

_____

Write the memory verse for this week: *I John 3: 2-3.*

_____

_____

_____

_____

_____

Write out three things you are grateful for today.

_____

_____

_____

Write out a prayer to God responding to today's lesson.

_____

_____

_____

_____

_____

Ask, "Lord, what do You want to say to me personally about my obedience to You?"

_____

_____

_____

_____

_____

Reflection: How did you experience God in a special way today or yesterday?

_____

_____

_____

_____

_____

Pray for: Someone to be saved _____ someone to disciple _____

Date	Prayer Requests Received Today	How and when answered? (Come back and follow up as needed)

Week Five

Day: _____ Date: _____ Time: _____

Scripture Reading: I John 5:6-15

What did you learn in today's reading? How will you apply it to your life?

_____

_____

_____

_____

_____

_____

What are you asking of God? Is it in His will or yours?

_____

_____

_____

_____

_____

What specific goal have you set for your Mental growth and refinement for this week? What is your progress?

_____

_____

Write the memory verse for this week: *I John 3: 2-3.*

_____

_____

_____

_____

_____

Write out three things you are grateful for today.

_____

_____

_____

Write out a prayer to God responding to today's lesson.

_____

_____

_____

_____

_____

Ask, "Lord, what do You want to say to me personally about the things that I have been asking of You?"

_____

_____

_____

_____

_____

_____

Reflection: How did you experience God in a special way today or yesterday?

_____

_____

_____

_____

_____

Pray for: Someone to be saved _____ someone to disciple _____

Date	Prayer Requests Received Today	How and when answered? (Come back and follow up as needed)

Week Five

Day: _____ Date: _____ Time: _____

Scripture Reading: I John 5:16-17

What did you learn in today's reading? How will you apply it to your life?

_____

_____

_____

_____

_____

What sin leads to death? How will you pray for those who are in sin?

_____

_____

_____

_____

_____

_____

What specific goal have you set for your Social/Emotional growth and refinement this week? What is your progress?

_____

_____

Write the memory verse *for this week: I John 3: 2-3.*

_____

_____

_____

_____

_____

Write out three things you are grateful for today.

_____

_____

_____

Write out a prayer to God responding to today's lesson.

_____

_____

_____

_____

_____

_____

Ask, "Lord, what do You want to say to me personally about how and who I need to pray for that is caught in a sin?"

_____

_____

_____

_____

_____

Reflection: How did you experience God in a special way today or yesterday?

_____

_____

_____

_____

Pray for: Someone to be saved _____ someone to disciple _____

Date	Prayer Requests Received Today	How and when answered? (Come back and follow up as needed)

Week Five

Day: _____ Date: _____ Time: _____

Scripture Reading: I John 5:18-21

What did you learn in today's reading? How will you apply it to your life?

_____

_____

_____

_____

_____

_____

Do you have any idols in your life? If so, what can you do to remove them from your life?

_____

_____

_____

_____

_____

What specific goal have you set for your Physical growth and resentment for this week? What is your progress?

_____

_____

Write the memory verse for this week: *I John 3: 2-3.*

_____

_____

_____

_____

Write out three things you are grateful for today.

_____

_____

_____

Write out a prayer to God responding to today's lesson.

_____

_____

_____

_____

_____

_____

Ask, "Lord, reveal to me any idols that I may have in my life and how to remove them."

_____

_____

_____

_____

_____

Reflection: How did you experience God in a special way today or yesterday?

_____

_____

_____

_____

Pray for: Someone to be saved _____ someone to disciple _____

Date	Prayer Requests Received Today	How and when answered? (Come back and follow up as needed)

Week Five

Day: _____ Date: _____ Time: _____

Lesson 5: Walk in Love

Scripture Reading: Ephesians 5:1-7

What did you learn in today's reading? How will you apply it to your life?

_____

_____

_____

_____

_____

_____

Are you an imitator of God or are you walking in immorality? How can you live out holiness?

_____

_____

_____

_____

_____

What specific goal have you set for your Financial growth and refinement for this week? What is your progress?

_____

_____

Write the memory verse for this week: *I John 3: 2-3.*

_____

_____

_____

_____

_____

Write out three things you are grateful for today.

_____

_____

_____

Write out a prayer to God responding to today's lesson.

_____

_____

_____

_____

_____

Ask, "Lord, what do You want to say to me personally about my walk with You and how I can learn to be more thankful?"

_____

_____

_____

_____

_____

Reflection: How did you experience God in a special way today or yesterday?

_____

_____

_____

_____

Pray for: Someone to be saved _____ someone to disciple _____

Date	Prayer Requests Received Today	How and when answered? (Come back and follow up as needed)

Notes

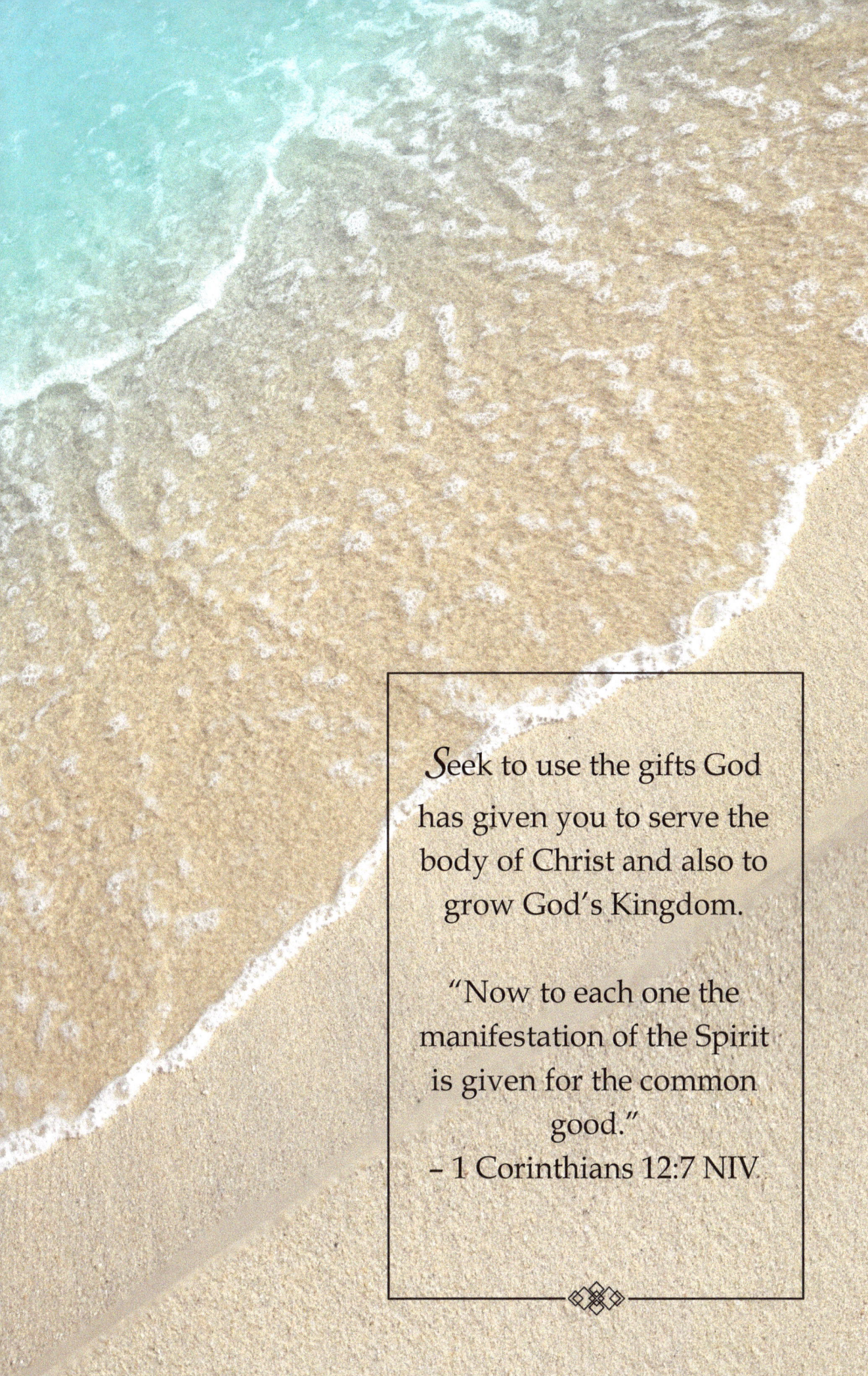

Seek to use the gifts God has given you to serve the body of Christ and also to grow God's Kingdom.

"Now to each one the manifestation of the Spirit is given for the common good."
– 1 Corinthians 12:7 NIV.

Church Sermon Notes

—◆—

Theme:

_____

_____

_____

Scriptures:

_____

_____

_____

Lessons:

_____

_____

_____

_____

_____

_____

Application:

_____

_____

_____

_____

_____

_____

Notes:

_____

_____

_____

_____

_____

Church Sermon Notes

Theme:

_____

_____

_____

Scriptures:

_____

_____

_____

Lessons:

_____

_____

_____

_____

_____

_____

Application:

_____

_____

_____

_____

_____

_____

Notes:

_____

_____

_____

_____

_____

Things to Remember from Week Five

Scriptures:

_____

_____

_____

Application:

_____

_____

_____

Goals Set:

_____

_____

_____

Memory Verse:

_____

_____

_____

Time with God:

_____

_____

_____

Reflection:

_____

_____

_____

Answered Prayers:

_____

_____

_____

Week Six

Love in Action

———◆———

Are you starting to see positive changes in your life? In this week, look for ways to show love in action, especially with your family and friends. Share with your accountability partner how you showed love in action and the response you received.

How did you show love?

_____

_____

_____

What was the person's response?

_____

_____

_____

This may be a challenging week for you but keep moving forward.

YOU CAN DO THIS!

Note: If you haven't yet, this is a quick reminder to go ahead and get Volume 2 so that once you finish Week Six, you can get started on the last six weeks of the study right away.

Write out your goals to keep them in mind until the new habit is formed. Make any needed adjustments.

Goals	Spiritual	Mental	Social/ Emotional	Physical	Financial
New Habit (What…be specific)					
Measurable Growth (How much and/or when)					
Period (daily, weekly, monthly)					

Week Six

Lesson 1: Walk in Light

Scripture Reading: Ephesians 5:8-14

What did you learn in today's reading? How will you apply it to your life?

_____

_____

_____

_____

_____

After meditating on this passage, what words of revelation came alive and spoke to your heart? How will you live it out?

_____

_____

_____

_____

_____

What specific goal have you set for your Spiritual growth and refinement for this week? What is your progress?

_____

_____

Write the memory verse for this week: *Isaiah 41:10.*

_____

_____

_____

_____

Write out three things you are grateful for today.

_____

_____

_____

Write out a prayer to God responding to today's lesson.

_____

_____

_____

_____

_____

_____

Ask, "Lord, what do You want to say to me personally about what pleases You?"

_____

_____

_____

_____

_____

_____

Reflection: How did you experience God in a special way today or yesterday?

_____

_____

_____

_____

Pray for: Someone to be saved _____ someone to disciple _____

Date	Prayer Requests Received Today	How and when answered? (Come back and follow up as needed)

Week Six

Day: _____ Date: _____ Time: _____

Lesson 2: Walk in Wisdom

Scripture Reading: Ephesians 5:15-20

What did you learn in today's reading? How will you apply it to your life?

_____

_____

_____

_____

_____

_____

What word(s) of revelation came alive and spoke to your heart? How will you live it out?

_____

_____

_____

_____

_____

_____

What specific goal have you set for your Mental growth and refinement for this week? What is your progress?

_____

_____

_____

Write the memory verse for this week: *Isaiah 41:10.*

_____

_____

_____

_____

Write out three things you are grateful for today.

_____

_____

_____

Write out a prayer to God responding to today's lesson.

_____

_____

_____

_____

_____

_____

Ask, "Lord, what do You want to say to me personally about how to be filled with the Holy Spirit?"

_____

_____

_____

_____

_____

_____

Reflection: How did you experience God in a special way today or yesterday?

_____

_____

_____

_____

Pray for: Someone to be saved _____ someone to disciple _____

Date	Prayer Requests Received Today	How and when answered? (Come back and follow up as needed)

Week Six

Day: _____ Date: _____ Time: _____

Lesson 3: Marriage

Scripture Reading: Ephesians 5:21-33

What did you learn in today's reading? How will you apply it to your life?

_____

_____

_____

_____

_____

_____

If you are married, are you being submissive/respectful to your spouse and loving them? How will you show it?

_____

_____

_____

_____

_____

What specific goal have you set for your Social/Emotional growth and refinement for this week? What is your progress?

_____

_____

Write the memory verse for this week: *Isaiah 41:10.*

_____

_____

_____

_____

Write out three things you are grateful for today.

_____

_____

_____

Write out a prayer to God responding to today's lesson.

_____

_____

_____

_____

_____

_____

Ask, "Lord, what do You want to say to me personally about my intimate relationship with You or my spouse?"

_____

_____

_____

_____

_____

Reflection: How did you experience God in a special way today or yesterday?

_____

_____

_____

_____

Pray for: Someone to be saved _____ someone to disciple _____

Date	Prayer Requests Received Today	How and when answered? (Come back and follow up as needed)

Week Six

Day: _____ Date: _____ Time: _____

Lesson 4: Christian Home

Scripture Reading: Colossians 3:18-4:1

What did you learn in today's reading? How will you apply it to your life?

_____

_____

_____

_____

_____

_____

How do you relate to others as God desires?

_____

_____

_____

_____

_____

_____

What specific goal have you set for your Physical growth and refinement for this week? What is your progress?

_____

_____

Write the memory verse for this week: *Isaiah 41:10.*

_____

_____

_____

_____

Write out three things you are grateful for today.

_____

_____

_____

Write out a prayer to God responding to today's lesson.

_____

_____

_____

_____

_____

_____

Ask, "Lord, what do You want to say to me personally about how I relate other people in my family?"

_____

_____

_____

_____

_____

_____

Reflection: How did you experience God in a special way today or yesterday?

_____

_____

_____

_____

Pray for: Someone to be saved _____ someone to disciple _____

Date	Prayer Requests Received Today	How and when answered? (Come back and follow up as needed)

Week Six

Day: _____ Date: _____ Time: _____

Scripture Reading: Colossians 4:2-6

What did you learn in today's reading? How will you apply it to your life?

_____

_____

_____

_____

_____

_____

How are you making every opportunity to communicate with others the hope you have in Christ? Is it seasoned with salt?

_____

_____

_____

_____

_____

What specific goal have you set for your Financial growth and refinement for this week? What is your progress?

_____

_____

Write the memory verse for this week: *Isaiah 41:10.*

_____

_____

_____

_____

Write out three things you are grateful for today.

_____

_____

_____

Write out a prayer to God responding to today's lesson.

_____

_____

_____

_____

_____

_____

Ask, "Lord, what do You want to say to me personally about my prayer life?"

_____

_____

_____

_____

_____

Reflection: How did you experience God in a special way today or yesterday?

_____

_____

_____

_____

Pray for: Someone to be saved _____ someone to disciple _____

Date	Prayer Requests Received Today	How and when answered? (Come back and follow up as needed)

Notes

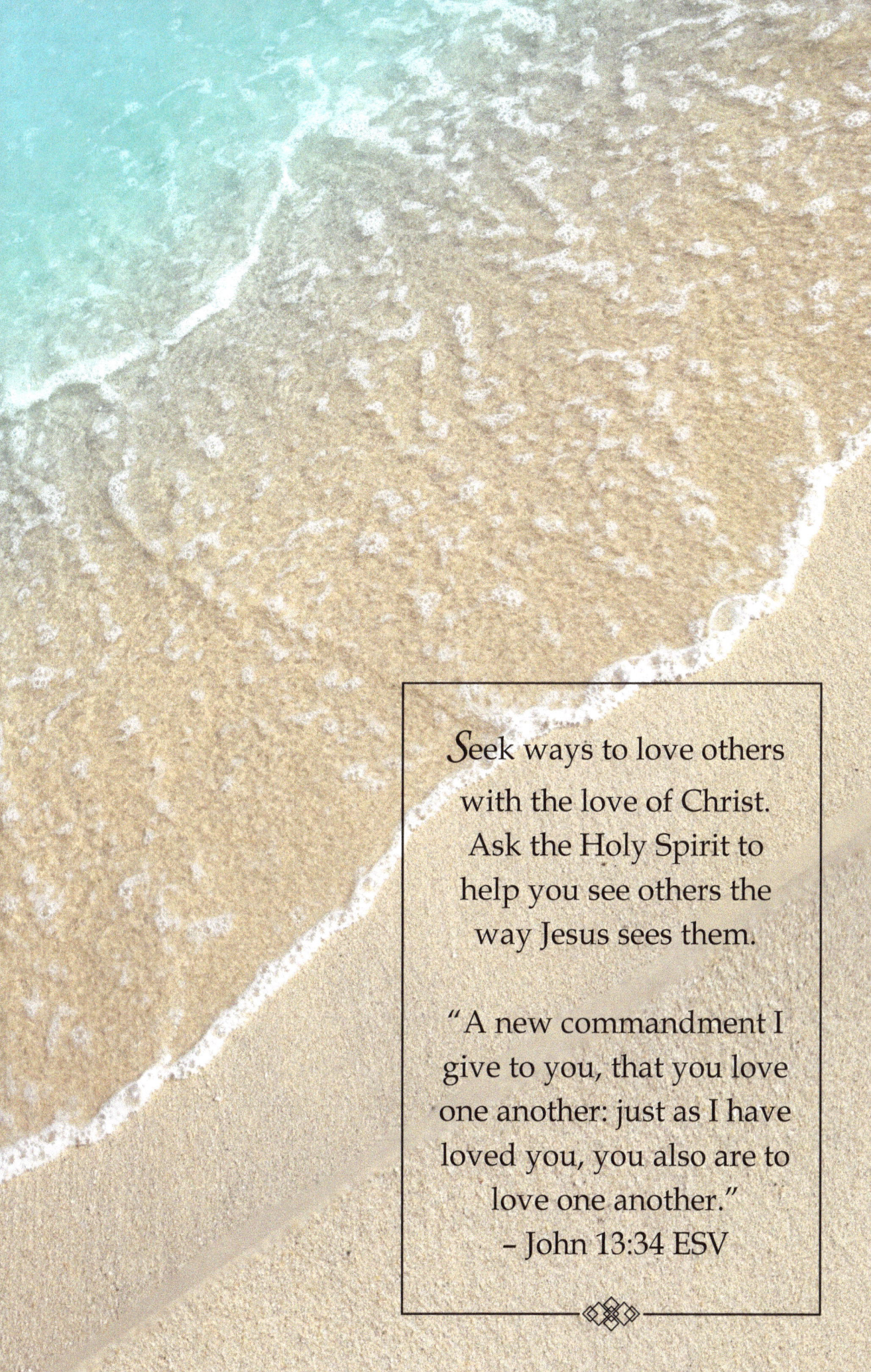

Seek ways to love others
with the love of Christ.
Ask the Holy Spirit to
help you see others the
way Jesus sees them.

"A new commandment I
give to you, that you love
one another: just as I have
loved you, you also are to
love one another."
– John 13:34 ESV

Church Sermon Notes

———◆——

Theme:

_____

_____

_____

Scriptures:

_____

_____

_____

Lessons:

_____

_____

_____

_____

_____

_____

Application:

_____

_____

_____

_____

_____

Notes:

_____

_____

_____

_____

_____

Things to Remember from Week Six

Scriptures:

_____

_____

_____

Application:

_____

_____

_____

Goals Set:

_____

_____

_____

Memory Verse:

_____

_____

_____

Time with God:

_____

_____

_____

Reflection:

_____

_____

_____

Answered Prayers:

_____

_____

_____

Mid-Way Self-Evaluation

My life as of _____, 20_____

Spiritual	Yes	No	How Often
Do I read God's Word each day?			
Do I pray for my family, others, and myself?			
Am I attending a Bible-based Church?			
Do I testify about God to others?			
Mental			
Do I have a cheerful outlook?			
Do I listen to, watch, and read things that are uplifting and encouraging?			
Do I speak and react to others in a kind manner?			
Social/Emotional			
Do I honor and respect my spouse and family?			
Am I learning from a mentor or coach?			
Am I involved in a small group/community?			
Physical			
Do I eat/drink the right things each day?			
Do I exercise every day?			
Do I get enough rest daily?			
Financial			
Do I give to the Lord?			
Am I in debt?			
Do I save for an emergency fund?			
Total of columns			

Six-Week Reflection

Take some time to reflect on key things that you learned that God revealed to you in the past six weeks, or that you want to carry with you moving forward.

_____

_____

_____

_____

_____

_____

Was there anything that seemed to be a repeating focus during each of the past six weeks?

_____

_____

_____

_____

_____

In what ways have you grown in your relationship with God and in recognizing His voice?

_____

_____

_____

_____

_____

_____

Once you've taken time to reflect on your journey so far, continue with Week Seven to complete all twelve weeks of the study.

Week Seven

Led by the Holy Spirit

---◆---

In this week, allow the Holy Spirit to lead you. Give up your agenda and be faithful to obey the Spirit's leadership. In Galatians 5:16-18, NIV *Life Application Bible* commentary (1991) states:

> Being led by the Holy Spirit involves the desire to hear, the readiness to obey God's Word, and the sensitivity to discern between your feelings and His promptings. Live each day controlled and guided by the Holy Spirit. Then the words of Christ will be in your mind, the love of Christ will be behind your actions, and the power of Christ will help you control your selfish desires.

Share with your accountability partner what the Holy Spirit may have led you to do. Did you follow through faithfully? How?

Write out your goals from last week to keep them in mind until the new habit is formed. Make any needed adjustments.

Goals	Spiritual	Mental	Social/ Emotional	Physical	Financial
New Habit (What…be specific)					
Measurable Growth (How much and/or when)					
Period (daily, weekly, monthly)					

Week Seven

Day: _____ Date: _____ Time: _____

Scripture Reading: Galatians 5:13-18

What did you learn in today's reading? How will you apply it to your life?

_____

_____

_____

_____

_____

_____

Who may have cut in on you and kept you from obeying the truth? How did they do this? What can you do now?

_____

_____

_____

_____

_____

_____

What specific goal have you set for your Spiritual growth and refinement for this week? What is your progress?

_____

_____

Write the memory verse for this week: *Romans 8:14.*

_____

_____

_____

Write out three things you are grateful for today.

_____

_____

_____

Write out a prayer to God responding to today's lesson.

_____

_____

_____

_____

_____

_____

Ask, "Lord, what do You want to say to me personally about serving others?"

_____

_____

_____

_____

_____

_____

Reflection: How did you experience God in a special way today or yesterday?

_____

_____

_____

_____

Pray for: Someone to be saved _____ someone to disciple _____

Date	Prayer Requests Received Today	How and when answered? (Come back and follow up as needed)

Week Seven

Day: _____ Date: _____ Time: _____

Scripture Reading: Galatians 5:19-26

What did you learn in today's reading? How will you apply it to your life?

_____

_____

_____

_____

_____

_____

Is there a sinful nature that is active in your life right now? If so, what will you do to stop that activity in your life?

_____

_____

_____

_____

_____

_____

What specific goal have you set for your Mental growth and refinement for this week? What is your progress?

_____

_____

Write the memory verse for this week: *Romans 8:14.*

_____

_____

_____

Write out three things you are grateful for today.

_____

_____

_____

Write out a prayer to God responding to today's lesson.

_____

_____

_____

_____

_____

_____

Ask, "Lord, what do You want to say to me personally about the fruit of the Spirit in my life?"

_____

_____

_____

_____

_____

Reflection: How did you experience God in a special way today or yesterday?

_____

_____

_____

_____

Pray for: Someone to be saved _____ someone to disciple _____

Date	Prayer Requests Received Today	How and when answered? (Come back and follow up as needed)

Week Seven

Day: _____ Date: _____ Time: _____

Scripture Reading: Gospel of John 14:1-6

What did you learn in today's reading? How will you apply it to your life?

_____

_____

_____

_____

_____

_____

After meditating on this passage, what word(s) of revelation came alive and spoke to your heart? How will you live it out?

_____

_____

_____

_____

_____

_____

What specific goal have you set for your Social/Emotional growth and refinement for this week? What is your progress?

_____

_____

Write the memory verse for this week: *Romans 8:14.*

_____

_____

_____

Write out three things you are grateful for today.

_____

_____

_____

Write out a prayer to God responding to today's lesson.

_____

_____

_____

_____

_____

_____

Ask, "Lord, what do You want to say to me personally about the area of life I need to trust You with more?"

_____

_____

_____

_____

_____

_____

Reflection: How did you experience God in a special way today or yesterday?

_____

_____

_____

_____

Pray for: Someone to be saved _____ someone to disciple _____

Date	Prayer Requests Received Today	How and when answered? (Come back and follow up as needed)

Week Seven

Day: _____ Date: _____ Time: _____

Scripture Reading: Gospel of John 14:7-11

What did you learn in today's reading? How will you apply it to your life?

_____

_____

_____

_____

_____

_____

What do you believe about the Father?

_____

_____

_____

_____

_____

_____

What specific goal have you set for your Physical growth and refinement for this week? What is your progress?

_____

_____

Write the memory verse for this week: *Romans 8:14.*

_____

_____

_____

Write out three things you are grateful for today.

_____

_____

_____

Write out a prayer to God responding to today's lesson.

_____

_____

_____

_____

_____

_____

Ask, "Lord, what do You want to say to me personally about how You show Yourself to me?"

_____

_____

_____

_____

_____

Reflection: How did you experience God in a special way today or yesterday?

_____

_____

_____

_____

Pray for: Someone to be saved _____ someone to disciple _____

Date	Prayer Requests Received Today	How and when answered? (Come back and follow up as needed)

Week Seven

Day: _____ Date: _____ Time: _____

Scripture Reading: Gospel of John 14:12-14

What did you learn in today's reading? How will you apply it to your life?

_____

_____

_____

_____

_____

_____

What is God asking you to do? How will you live it out?

_____

_____

_____

_____

_____

_____

What specific goal have you set for your Financial growth and refinement for this week? What is your progress?

_____

_____

Write the memory verse for this week: *Romans 8:14.*

_____

_____

_____

Write out three things you are grateful for today.

_____

_____

_____

Write out a prayer to God responding to today's lesson.

_____

_____

_____

_____

_____

_____

Ask, "Lord, what do You want to say to me personally about the things I ask of You to do?"

_____

_____

_____

_____

_____

_____

Reflection: How did you experience God in a special way today or yesterday?

_____

_____

_____

_____

Pray for: Someone to be saved _____ someone to disciple _____

Date	Prayer Requests Received Today	How and when answered? (Come back and follow up as needed)

Notes

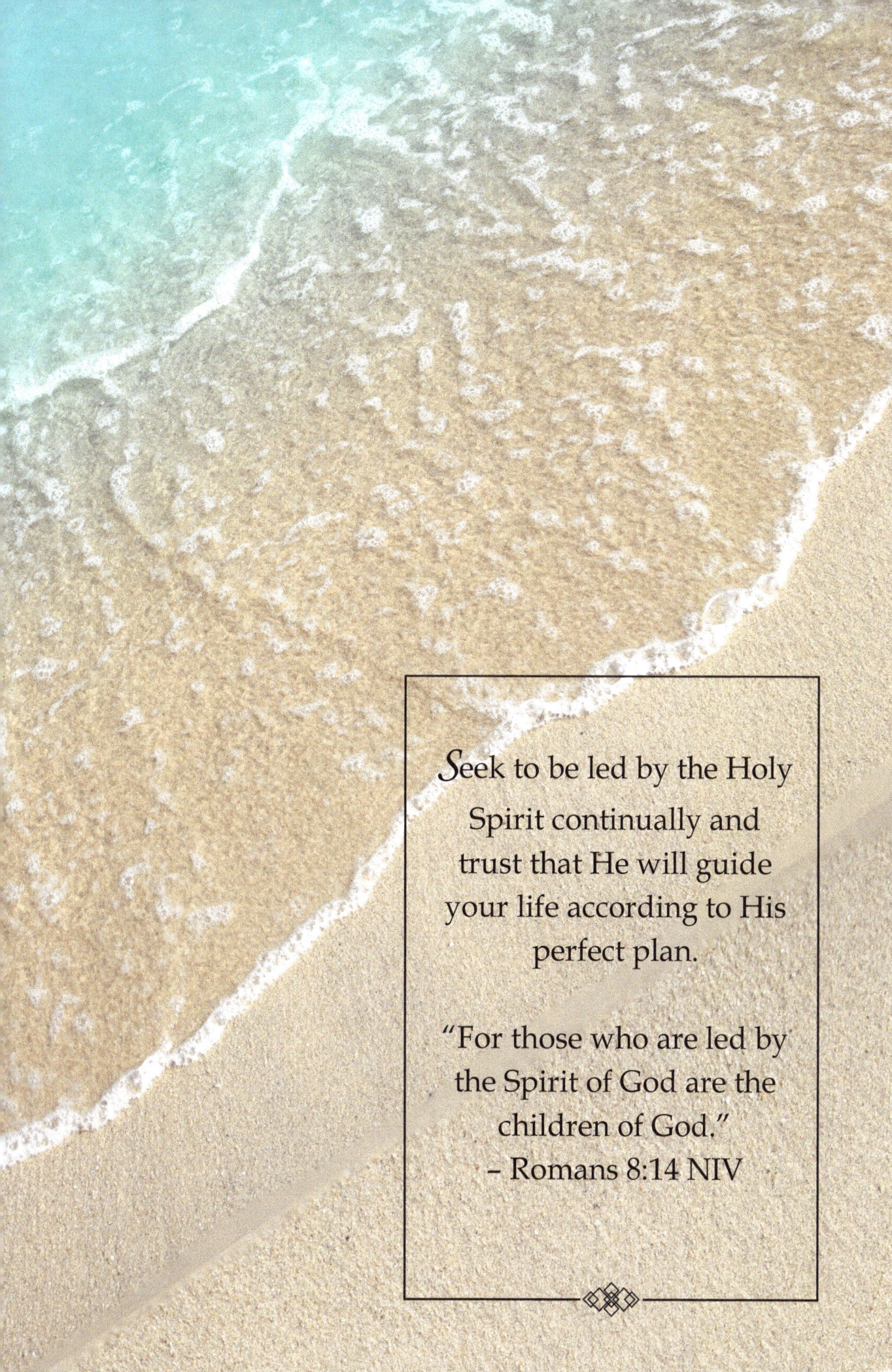

Seek to be led by the Holy
Spirit continually and
trust that He will guide
your life according to His
perfect plan.

"For those who are led by
the Spirit of God are the
children of God."
– Romans 8:14 NIV

Church Sermon Notes

Theme:

_____

_____

_____

Scriptures:

_____

_____

_____

Lessons:

_____

_____

_____

_____

_____

Application:

_____

_____

_____

_____

_____

Notes:

_____

_____

_____

_____

_____

Things to Remember from Week Seven

———◆———

Scriptures:

_____

_____

_____

Application:

_____

_____

_____

Goals Set:

_____

_____

_____

Memory Verse:

_____

_____

_____

Time with God:

_____

_____

_____

Reflection:

_____

_____

_____

Answered Prayers:

_____

_____

_____

Week Eight

Trust & Believe

———◆-◆———

In this week, trust and believe in the Holy Spirit's leadership. He may reveal something that does not seem possible. However, with God, all things are possible.

Share with your accountability partner what the Holy Spirit may have led you to do. Was your faith evaluated to let God lead in this situation or direction? How?

_____

_____

_____

_____

_____

_____

Write out your goals from last week to keep them in mind until the new habit is formed. Make any needed adjustments.

Goals	Spiritual	Mental	Social/ Emotional	Physical	Financial
New Habit (What…be specific)					
Measurable Growth (How much and/or when)					
Period (daily, weekly, monthly)					

Week Eight

Day: _____ Date: _____ Time: _____

Scripture Reading: Gospel of John 14:15-18

What did you learn in today's reading? How will you apply it to your life?

_____

_____

_____

_____

_____

_____

How are you showing that you love Jesus?

_____

_____

_____

_____

_____

_____

What specific goal have you set for your Spiritual growth and refinement for this week? What is your progress?

_____

_____

Write the memory verse for this week: *Proverbs 3:5-6.*

_____

_____

_____

_____

Write out three things you are grateful for today.

_____

_____

_____

Write out a prayer to God responding to today's lesson.

_____

_____

_____

_____

_____

_____

Ask, "Lord, what do You want to say to me personally about the way I obey Your commands?"

_____

_____

_____

_____

_____

_____

Reflection: How did you experience God in a special way today or yesterday?

_____

_____

_____

_____

Pray for: Someone to be saved _____ someone to disciple _____

Date	Prayer Requests Received Today	How and when answered? (Come back and follow up as needed)

Week Eight

Day: _____ Date: _____ Time: _____

Scripture Reading: Gospel of John 14:19-24

What did you learn in today's reading? How will you apply it to your life?

_____

_____

_____

_____

_____

_____

How will Jesus show Himself to you?

_____

_____

_____

_____

_____

_____

What specific goal have you set for your Mental growth and refinement for this week? What is your progress?

_____

_____

Write the memory verse for this week: *Proverbs 3:5-6.*

_____

_____

_____

_____

Write out three things you are grateful for today.

_____

_____

_____

Write out a prayer to God responding to today's lesson.

_____

_____

_____

_____

_____

_____

Ask, "Lord, what do You want to say to me personally about how You show Yourself to me?"

_____

_____

_____

_____

_____

Reflection: How did you experience God in a special way today or yesterday?

_____

_____

_____

_____

Pray for: Someone to be saved _____ someone to disciple _____

Date	Prayer Requests Received Today	How and when answered? (Come back and follow up as needed)

Week Eight

Day: _____ Date: _____ Time: _____

Scripture Reading: Gospel of John 14:25-31

What did you learn in today's reading? How will you apply it to your life?

_____

_____

_____

_____

_____

After meditating on this passage, what word(s) of revelation came alive and spoke to your heart? How will you live it out?

_____

_____

_____

_____

_____

_____

_____

What specific goal have you set for your Social/Emotional growth and refinement for this week? What is your progress?

_____

_____

Write the memory verse for this week: *Proverbs 3:5-6.*

_____

_____

_____

Write out three things you are grateful for today.

_____

_____

_____

Write out a prayer to God responding to today's lesson.

_____

_____

_____

_____

_____

_____

Ask, "Lord, what do You want to say to me personally about how to receive peace in my life?"

_____

_____

_____

_____

_____

_____

Reflection: How did you experience God in a special way today or yesterday?

_____

_____

_____

_____

Pray for: Someone to be saved _____ someone to disciple _____

Date	Prayer Requests Received Today	How and when answered? (Come back and follow up as needed)

Week Eight

Day: _____ Date: _____ Time: _____

Scripture Reading: Gospel of John 15:1-8

What did you learn in today's reading? How will you apply it to your life?

_____

_____

_____

_____

_____

_____

How are you staying connected to the vine?

_____

_____

_____

_____

_____

_____

What specific goal have you set for your Physical growth and refinement for this week? What is your progress?

_____

_____

Write the memory verse for this week: *Proverbs 3:5-6.*

_____

_____

_____

_____

Write out three things you are grateful for today.

_____

_____

_____

Write out a prayer to God responding to today's lesson.

_____

_____

_____

_____

_____

_____

Ask, "Lord, what do You want to say to me personally about being connected to the vine?"

_____

_____

_____

_____

_____

_____

Reflection: How did you experience God in a special way today or yesterday?

_____

_____

_____

_____

Pray for: Someone to be saved _____ someone to disciple _____

Date	Prayer Requests Received Today	How and when answered? (Come back and follow up as needed)

Week Eight

Day: _____ Date: _____ Time: _____

Scripture Reading: Gospel of John 15:9-17

What did you learn in today's reading? How will you apply it to your life?

_____

_____

_____

_____

_____

_____

How can you develop joy in your heart?

_____

_____

_____

_____

_____

What specific goal have you set for your Financial growth and refinement for this week? What is your progress?

_____

_____

_____

Write the memory verse for this week: *Proverbs 3:5-6.*

_____

_____

_____

_____

Write out three things you are grateful for today.

_____

_____

_____

Write out a prayer to God responding to today's lesson.

_____

_____

_____

_____

_____

_____

_____

Ask, "Lord, what do You want to say to me personally about the kind of fruit that will last?"

_____

_____

_____

_____

_____

_____

_____

Reflection: How did you experience God in a special way today or yesterday?

_____

_____

_____

_____

Pray for: Someone to be saved _____ someone to disciple _____

Date	Prayer Requests Received Today	How and when answered? (Come back and follow up as needed)

Notes

As Holy Spirit leads, it will challenge your faith, and always be for good and for growth. Walk in faith.

"For we live by faith, not by sight." – 2 Corinthians 5:7 ESV

"Since we live by the Spirit, let us keep in step with the Spirit." – Galatians 5:25 NIV

Church Sermon Notes

Theme:

_____

_____

_____

Scriptures:

_____

_____

_____

Lessons:

_____

_____

_____

_____

_____

_____

Application:

_____

_____

_____

_____

_____

_____

Notes:

_____

_____

_____

_____

_____

Things to Remember from Week Eight

Scriptures:

_____

_____

_____

Application:

_____

_____

_____

Goals Set:

_____

_____

_____

Memory Verse:

_____

_____

_____

Time with God:

_____

_____

_____

Reflection:

_____

_____

_____

Answered Prayers:

_____

_____

_____

Week Nine

Receiving Answers

Are you starting to see more changes in your life? In this week, be prepared to start receiving answers to your challenges. God may bring a person into your life that will help you achieve your goals. Share with your accountability/prayer partner any answers to your challenges.

Write out your goals from last week to keep them in mind until the new habit is formed. Make any needed adjustments.

Goals	Spiritual	Mental	Social/ Emotional	Physical	Financial
New Habit (What…be specific)					
Measurable Growth (How much and/or when)					
Period (daily, weekly, monthly)					

Week Nine

Day: _____ Date: _____ Time: _____

Scripture Reading: Gospel of John 15:18-25

What did you learn in today's reading? How will you apply it to your life?

_____

_____

_____

_____

_____

_____

Have you ever felt like you were hated by those around you? What did you do about it?

_____

_____

_____

_____

_____

_____

What specific goal have you set for your Spiritual growth and refinement for this week? What is your progress?

_____

_____

Write the memory verse for this week: *John 16:24.*

_____

_____

_____

Write out three things you are grateful for today

_____

_____

_____

Write out a prayer to God responding to today's lesson.

_____

_____

_____

_____

_____

_____

Ask, "Lord, what do You want to say to me personally about being persecuted?"

_____

_____

_____

_____

_____

_____

Reflection: How did you experience God in a special way today or yesterday?

_____

_____

_____

_____

Pray for: Someone to be saved _____ someone to disciple _____

Date	Prayer Requests Received Today	How and when answered? (Come back and follow up as needed)

Week Nine

Day: _____ Date: _____ Time: _____

Scripture Reading: Gospel of John 15:26-16:4

What did you learn in today's reading? How will you apply it to your life?

_____

_____

_____

_____

_____

_____

How do you testify about Jesus?

_____

_____

_____

_____

_____

_____

What specific goal have you set for your Mental growth and refinement for this week? What is your progress?

_____

_____

Write the memory verse for this week: *John 16:24.*

_____

_____

Write out three things you are grateful for today.

_____

_____

_____

Write out a prayer to God responding to today's lesson.

_____

_____

_____

_____

_____

_____

Ask, "Lord, what do You want to say to me personally about the Spirit of truth?"

_____

_____

_____

_____

_____

Reflection: How did you experience God in a special way today or yesterday?

_____

_____

_____

_____

Pray for: Someone to be saved _____ someone to disciple _____

Date	Prayer Requests Received Today	How and when answered? (Come back and follow up as needed)

Week Nine

Day: _____ Date: _____ Time: _____

Scripture Reading: Gospel of John 16:5-15

What did you learn in today's reading? How will you apply it to your life?

_____

_____

_____

_____

_____

_____

Is the Holy Spirit convicting you of guilt, sin, or righteousness? What can you do to make a change in your life?

_____

_____

_____

_____

_____

_____

What specific goal have you set for your Social/Emotional growth and refinement for this week? What is your progress?

_____

_____

Write the memory verse for this week: *John 16:24.*

_____

_____

_____

Write out three things you are grateful for today.

_____

_____

_____

Write out a prayer to God responding to today's lesson.

_____

_____

_____

_____

_____

_____

_____

Ask, "Lord, what do You want to say to me personally about belonging to You?"

_____

_____

_____

_____

_____

_____

_____

Reflection: How did you experience God in a special way today or yesterday?

_____

_____

_____

_____

Pray for: Someone to be saved _____ someone to disciple _____

Date	Prayer Requests Received Today	How and when answered? (Come back and follow up as needed)

Week Nine

Day: _____ Date: _____ Time: _____

Scripture Reading: Gospel of John 16:16-24

What did you learn in today's reading? How will you apply it to your life?

_____

_____

_____

_____

_____

_____

After meditating on this passage, what must change in your life, so you are living as God wants? How will you live it out?

_____

_____

_____

_____

_____

_____

What specific goal have you set for your Physical growth and refinement for this week? What is your progress?

_____

_____

Write the memory verse for this week: *John 16:24.*

_____

_____

_____

Write out three things you are grateful for today.

_____

_____

_____

Write out a prayer to God responding to today's lesson.

_____

_____

_____

_____

_____

_____

Ask, "Lord, what do You want to say to me personally about how to have joy in my life, no matter my circumstances?"

_____

_____

_____

_____

_____

Reflection: How did you experience God in a special way today or yesterday?

_____

_____

_____

_____

Pray for: Someone to be saved _____ someone to disciple _____

Date	Prayer Requests Received Today	How and when answered? (Come back and follow up as needed)

Week Nine

Day: _____ Date: _____ Time: _____

Scripture Reading: Gospel of John 16:25-33

What did you learn in today's reading? How will you apply it to your life?

_____

_____

_____

_____

_____

_____

What area in your life are you trying to overcome? Have you given it over to Jesus?

_____

_____

_____

_____

_____

_____

What specific goal have you set for your Financial growth and refinement for this week? What is your progress?

_____

_____

Write the memory verse for this week: *John 16:24.*

_____

_____

_____

Write out three things you are grateful for today.

_____

_____

_____

Write out a prayer to God responding to today's lesson.

_____

_____

_____

_____

_____

_____

Ask, "Lord, what do You want to say to me personally about overcoming with victory?"

_____

_____

_____

_____

_____

_____

Reflection: How did you experience God in a special way today or yesterday?

_____

_____

_____

_____

Pray for: Someone to be saved _____ someone to disciple _____

Date	Prayer Requests Received Today	How and when answered? (Come back and follow up as needed)

Notes

Take everything to the
Lord always and surrender
all things to Him.

"The righteous cry out, and
the Lord hears, and delivers
them from all their
troubles."
– Psalm 34:17 NASB

Church Sermon Notes

Theme:

_____

_____

_____

Scriptures:

_____

_____

_____

Lessons:

_____

_____

_____

_____

_____

_____

Application:

_____

_____

_____

_____

_____

Notes:

_____

_____

_____

_____

_____

Things to Remember from Week Nine

Scriptures:

_____

_____

_____

Application:

_____

_____

_____

Goals Set:

_____

_____

_____

Memory Verse:

_____

_____

_____

Time with God:

_____

_____

_____

Reflection:

_____

_____

_____

Answered Prayers:

_____

_____

_____

Week Ten

Pray Continually

---◆---

This week challenges you to pray more. In I Thessalonians 5:17, it says, "Pray continually."

Continue to lift your challenges, anxieties, or struggles to God in prayer, and thank Him for what He has been doing so far in your life. May He receive the glory! ☺ Share with your accountability partner any prayer requests that still need to be answered. Take time to pray together more intensely, specifically, and intentionally.

Write out your goals from last week to keep them in mind until the new habit is formed. Make any needed adjustments.

Goals	Spiritual	Mental	Social/ Emotional	Physical	Financial
New Habit (What…be specific)					
Measurable Growth (How much and/or when)					
Period (daily, weekly, monthly)					

Week Ten

Day: _____ Date: _____Time: _____

Scripture Reading: Gospel of John 17:1-5

What did you learn in today's reading? How will you apply it to your life?

_____

_____

_____

_____

_____

Do you know the One true God and Jesus whom He sent? What do you know about them?

_____

_____

_____

_____

_____

_____

What specific goal have you set for your Spiritual growth and refinement for this week? What is your progress?

_____

_____

Write the memory verse for this week: *I John 5:14-15,*

_____

_____

_____

_____

_____

_____

Write out three things you are grateful for today.

_____

_____

_____

Write out a prayer to God responding to today's lesson.

_____

_____

_____

_____

_____

_____

Ask, "Lord, what do You want to say to me personally about bringing glory to Your name?"

_____

_____

_____

_____

_____

_____

Reflection: How did you experience God in a special way today or yesterday?

_____

_____

_____

_____

Pray for: Someone to be saved _____ someone to disciple _____

Date	Prayer Requests Received Today	How and when answered? (Come back and follow up as needed)

Week Ten

Day: _____ Date: _____ Time: _____

Lesson 2: Jesus Prays for Disciples

Scripture Reading: Gospel of John 17:6-19

What did you learn in today's reading? How will you apply it to your life?

_____

_____

_____

_____

_____

_____

Does your life reveal Jesus' character and presence? How or why not?

_____

_____

_____

_____

_____

What specific goal have you set for your Mental growth and refinement for this week? What is your progress?

_____

_____

Write the memory verse for this week: *I John 5:14-15.*

_____

_____

_____

_____

_____

Write out three things you are grateful for today.

_____

_____

_____

Write out a prayer to God responding to today's lesson.

_____

_____

_____

_____

_____

_____

Ask, "Lord, what do You want to say to me personally about being sanctified?"

_____

_____

_____

_____

_____

Reflection: How did you experience God in a special way today or yesterday?

_____

_____

_____

_____

Pray for: Someone to be saved _____ someone to disciple _____

Date	Prayer Requests Received Today	How and when answered? (Come back and follow up as needed)

Week Ten

Day: _____ Date: _____ Time: _____

Scripture Reading: Gospel of John 17:20-26

What did you learn in today's reading? How will you apply it to your life?

_____

_____

_____

_____

_____

_____

How are you helping to unify the body of Christ?

_____

_____

_____

_____

_____

What specific goal have you set for your Social/Emotional growth and refinement for this week? What is your progress?

_____

_____

Write the memory verse for this week: *1 John 5:14-15.*

_____

_____

_____

_____

_____

_____

Write out three things you are grateful for today.

_____

_____

_____

Write out a prayer to God responding to today's lesson.

_____

_____

_____

_____

_____

_____

Ask, "Lord, what do You want to say to me personally about praying for other believers?"

_____

_____

_____

_____

_____

_____

Reflection: How did you experience God in a special way today or yesterday?

_____

_____

_____

_____

Pray for: Someone to be saved _____ someone to disciple _____

Date	Prayer Requests Received Today	How and when answered? (Come back and follow up as needed)

Week Ten

Day: _____ Date: _____ Time: _____

Scripture Reading: Romans 6:1-15

What did you learn in today's reading? How will you apply it to your life?

_____

_____

_____

_____

_____

How are you offering yourself as a living sacrifice to God?

_____

_____

_____

_____

_____

What specific goal have you set for your Physical growth and refinement for this week? What is your progress?

_____

_____

Write the memory verse for this week: *I John 5:14-15.*

_____

_____

_____

_____

_____

Write out three things you are grateful for today.

_____

_____

_____

Write out a prayer to God responding to today's lesson.

_____

_____

_____

_____

_____

_____

Ask, "Lord, what do You want to say to me personally about being alive in You?"

_____

_____

_____

_____

_____

_____

Reflection: How did you experience God in a special way today or yesterday?

_____

_____

_____

_____

Pray for: Someone to be saved _____ someone to disciple _____

Date	Prayer Requests Received Today	How and when answered? (Come back and follow up as needed)

Week Ten

Day: _____ Date: _____ Time: _____

Scripture Reading: Romans 6:16-23

What did you learn in today's reading? How will you apply it to your life?

_____

_____

_____

_____

_____

Are you serving your sinful nature or serving God? How do you rate your heart of obedience? Is it fully committed to God or half-hardheartedly serving Him?

_____

_____

_____

_____

_____

_____

What specific goal have you set for your Financial growth and refinement for this week? What is your progress?

_____

_____

Write the memory verse for this week: *I John 5:14-15.*

_____

_____

_____

_____

_____

_____

Write out three things you are grateful for today.

_____

_____

_____

Write out a prayer to God responding to today's lesson.

_____

_____

_____

_____

_____

_____

Ask, "Lord, what do You want to say to me personally about being fully committed to You?"

_____

_____

_____

_____

_____

_____

Reflection: How did you experience God in a special way today or yesterday?

_____

_____

_____

_____

Pray for: Someone to be saved _____ someone to disciple _____

Date	Prayer Requests Received Today	How and when answered? (Come back and follow up as needed)

Notes

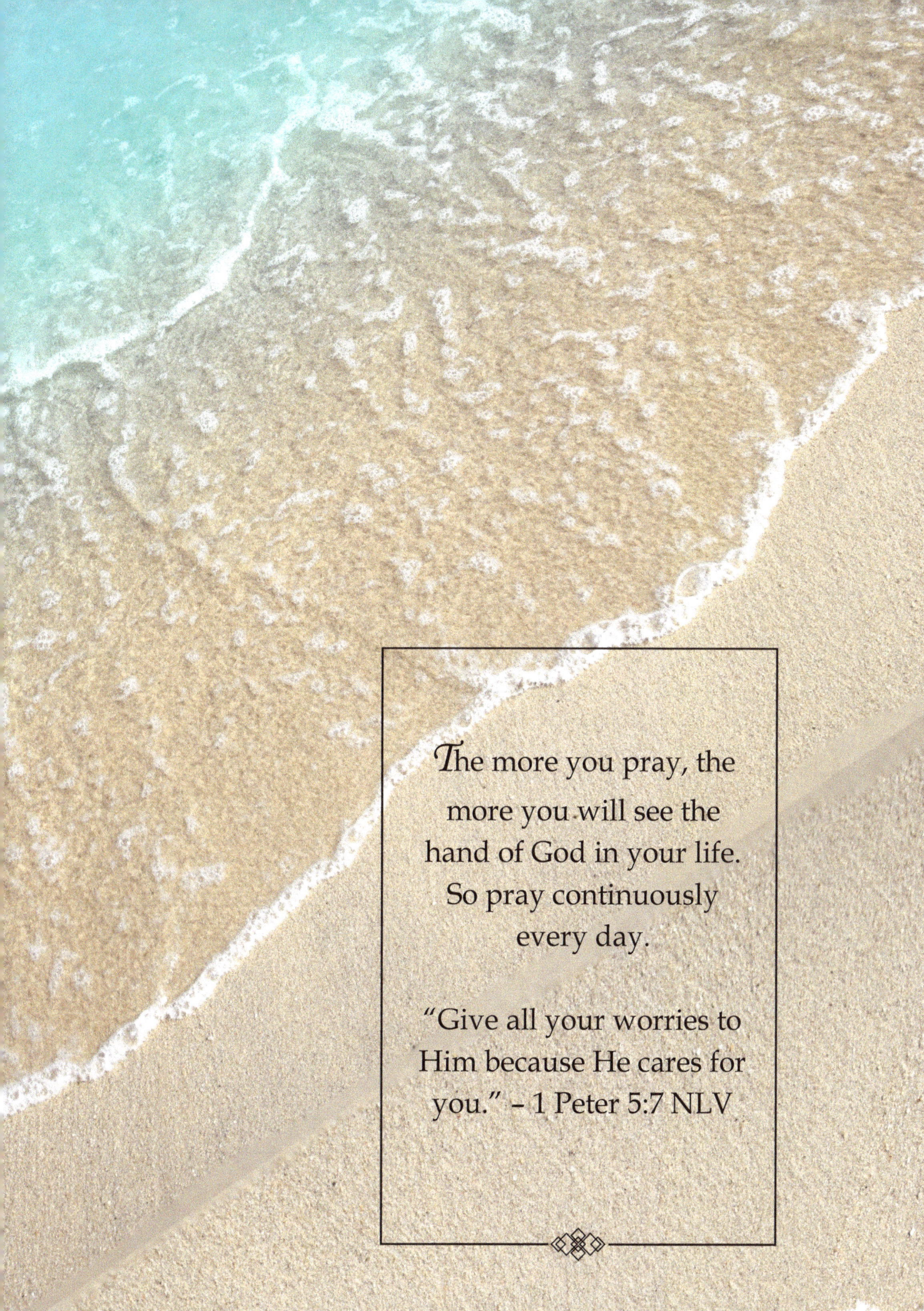

The more you pray, the
more you will see the
hand of God in your life.
So pray continuously
every day.

"Give all your worries to
Him because He cares for
you." – 1 Peter 5:7 NLV

Church Sermon Notes

Theme:

_____

_____

_____

Scriptures:

_____

_____

_____

Lessons:

_____

_____

_____

_____

_____

Application:

_____

_____

_____

_____

_____

Notes:

_____

_____

_____

_____

_____

Things to Remember from Week Ten

———◆———

Scriptures:

_____

_____

_____

Application:

_____

_____

_____

Goals Set:

_____

_____

_____

Memory Verse:

_____

_____

_____

Time with God:

_____

_____

Reflection:

_____

_____

_____

Answered Prayers:

_____

_____

_____

Week Eleven

Open Mind & Heart

---◆---

"Do not conform to the pattern of this world but be transformed by the renewing of your mind. Then you will be able to test and approve what God's will is — His good, pleasing and perfect will." Romans 12:2

This week you may see how God can place things in your life that reflect your change. Keep an open mind and heart to this change. Continue to lift your challenges, anxieties, or struggles to God in prayer, and thank Him for what He has been doing in your life. May He receive the glory! ☺ Share with your accountability partner anything God has revealed to you specifically.

Write out your goals from last week to keep them in mind until the new habit is formed. Make any needed adjustments.

Goals	Spiritual	Mental	Social/ Emotional	Physical	Financial
New Habit (What…be specific)					
Measurable Growth (How much and/or when)					
Period (daily, weekly, monthly)					

Week Eleven

Day: _____ Date: _____ Time: _____

Scripture Reading: Romans 8:1-11

What did you learn in today's reading? How will you apply it to your life?

_____

_____

_____

_____

_____

_____

Do you have your mind set on sinful nature or the Spirit? What can you do to be more Spirit-minded?

_____

_____

_____

_____

_____

_____

What specific goal have you set for your Spiritual growth and refinement for this week? What is your progress?

_____

_____

Write the memory verse for this week: *Romans 12:2.*

_____

_____

_____

Write out three things you are grateful for today.

_____

_____

_____

Write out a prayer to God responding to today's lesson.

_____

_____

_____

_____

_____

_____

Ask, "Lord, what do You want to say to me personally about where my focus needs to be?"

_____

_____

_____

_____

_____

Reflection: How did you experience God in a special way today or yesterday?

_____

_____

_____

_____

Pray for: Someone to be saved _____ someone to disciple _____

Date	Prayer Requests Received Today	How and when answered? (Come back and follow up as needed)

Week Eleven

Day: _____ Date: _____ Time: _____

Scripture Reading: Romans 8:12-17

What did you learn in today's reading? How will you apply it to your life?

_____

_____

_____

_____

_____

_____

Have you been adopted into the family of God? How will you cherish this blessing?

_____

_____

_____

_____

_____

_____

What specific goal have you set for your Mental growth and references for this week? What is your progress?

_____

_____

Write the memory verse for this week: *Romans 12:2.*

_____

_____

_____

Write out three things you are grateful for today.

_____

_____

_____

Write out a prayer to God responding to today's lesson.

_____

_____

_____

_____

_____

_____

Ask, "Lord, what do You want to say to me personally about being Your heir?"

_____

_____

_____

_____

_____

_____

Reflection: How did you experience God in a special way today or yesterday?

_____

_____

_____

_____

Pray for: Someone to be saved _____ someone to disciple _____

Date	Prayer Requests Received Today	How and when answered? (Come back and follow up as needed)

Week Eleven

Day: _____ Date: _____ Time: _____

Scripture Reading: Romans 8:18-30

What did you learn in today's reading? How will you apply it to your life?

_____

_____

_____

_____

_____

_____

What things can you do to be conformed into Christ-likeness?

_____

_____

_____

_____

_____

_____

What specific goal have you set for your Social/Emotional growth and refinement for this week? What is your progress?

_____

_____

Write the memory verse for this week: *Romans 12:2.*

_____

_____

_____

Write out three things you are grateful for today.

_____

_____

_____

Write out a prayer to God responding to today's lesson.

_____

_____

_____

_____

_____

_____

Ask, "Lord, what do You want to say to me personally about being conformed into the image of Christ?"

_____

_____

_____

_____

_____

_____

Reflection: How did you experience God in a special way today or yesterday?

_____

_____

_____

_____

Pray for: Someone to be saved _____ someone to disciple _____

Date	Prayer Requests Received Today	How and when answered? (Come back and follow up as needed)

Week Eleven

Day: _____ Date: _____ Time: _____

Scripture Reading: Romans 8:31-39

What did you learn in today's reading? How will you apply it to your life?

_____

_____

_____

_____

_____

_____

How are you more than a conqueror?

_____

_____

_____

_____

_____

_____

What specific goal have you set for your Physical growth and refinement for this week? What is your progress?

_____

_____

Write the memory verse for this week: *Romans 12:2.*

_____

_____

_____

Write out three things you are grateful for today.

_____

_____

_____

Write out a prayer to God responding to today's lesson.

_____

_____

_____

_____

_____

_____

Ask, "Lord, what do You want to say to me personally about Your love for me?"

_____

_____

_____

_____

_____

Reflection: How did you experience God in a special way today or yesterday?

_____

_____

_____

_____

Pray for: Someone to be saved _____ someone to disciple _____

Date	Prayer Requests Received Today	How and when answered? (Come back and follow up as needed)

Week Eleven

Day: _____ Date: _____Time: _____

Scripture Reading: Romans 12:1-2

What did you learn in today's reading? How will you apply it to your life?

_____

_____

_____

_____

_____

_____

Are you being transformed in your mind? If so, what changes have you made?

_____

_____

_____

_____

_____

_____

What specific goal have you set for your Financial growth and refinement for this week? What is your progress?

_____

_____

Write the memory verse for this week: *Romans 12:2.*

_____

_____

_____

Write out three things you are grateful for today.

_____

_____

_____

Write out a prayer to God responding to today's lesson.

_____

_____

_____

_____

_____

_____

Ask, "Lord, what do You want to say to me personally about the renewing of the mind?"

_____

_____

_____

_____

_____

_____

Reflection: How did you experience God in a special way today or yesterday?

_____

_____

_____

_____

Pray for: Someone to be saved _____ someone to disciple _____

Date	Prayer Requests Received Today	How and when answered? (Come back and follow up as needed)

Notes

Pray and seek out the mind of Christ, and you will have peace, hope, joy, and love.

"Finally, brothers and sisters, whatever is true, whatever is noble, whatever is right, whatever is pure, whatever is lovely, whatever is admirable—if anything is excellent or praiseworthy— think about such things."
– Philippians 4:8 NIV

Church Sermon Notes

Theme:

_____

_____

_____

Scriptures:

_____

_____

_____

Lessons:

_____

_____

_____

_____

_____

Application:

_____

_____

_____

_____

_____

Notes:

_____

_____

_____

_____

_____

Things to Remember from Week Eleven

———◆———

Scriptures:

_____

_____

_____

Application:

_____

_____

_____

Goals Set:

_____

_____

_____

Memory Verse:

_____

_____

_____

Time with God:

_____

_____

_____

Reflection:

_____

_____

_____

Answered Prayers:

_____

_____

_____

Week Twelve

Breakthrough

———————◆———————

In this week, be prepared for breakthroughs with your challenges if you haven't already been experiencing them. It may be difficult for you to do, but perseverance has its rewards. **At the end of this study, you will find a final self-evaluation form. Please take time to fill out and notice the changes that have taken place in your life from your first self-evaluation.** Share with your accountability partner all the changes you have seen take place in your life.

Write out your goals from last week to keep them in mind until the new habit is formed. Make any needed adjustments.

Goals	Spiritual	Mental	Social/ Emotional	Physical	Financial
New Habit (What…be specific)					
Measurable Growth (How much and/or when)					
Period (daily, weekly, monthly)					

Week Twelve

Day: _____ Date: _____ Time: _____

Scripture Reading: Romans 12:3-8

What did you learn in today's reading? How will you apply it to your life?

_____

_____

_____

_____

_____

Do you know what spiritual gifts God has placed within you? How are you using them for His glory? (Reference Week 5 as needed; consider what the Lord has revealed and worked in you over the last 12 weeks.)

_____

_____

_____

_____

_____

_____

What specific goal have you set for your Spiritual growth and refinement for this week? What is your progress?

_____

_____

Write the memory verse for this week: *1 Corinthians 15:57.*

_____

_____

_____

Write out three things you are grateful for today.

_____

_____

_____

Write out a prayer to God responding to today's lesson.

_____

_____

_____

_____

_____

_____

_____

Ask, "Lord, what do You want to say to me personally about the gifts You have placed in me?"

_____

_____

_____

_____

_____

_____

_____

Reflection: How did you experience God in a special way today or yesterday?

_____

_____

_____

_____

Pray for: Someone to be saved _____ someone to disciple _____

Date	Prayer Requests Received Today	How and when answered? (Come back and follow up as needed)

Week Twelve

Day: _____ Date: _____ Time: _____

Scripture Reading: Romans 12:9-21

What did you learn in today's reading? How will you apply it to your life?

_____

_____

_____

_____

_____

_____

How are you showing love in action?

_____

_____

_____

_____

_____

_____

What specific goal have you set for your Mental growth and refinement for this week? What is your progress?

_____

_____

Write the memory verse for this week: *1 Corinthians 15:57.*

_____

_____

_____

Write out three things you are grateful for today.

_____

_____

_____

Write out a prayer to God responding to today's lesson.

_____

_____

_____

_____

_____

_____

Ask, "Lord, what do You want to say to me personally about putting sincere love in action?"

_____

_____

_____

_____

_____

_____

Reflection: How did you experience God in a special way today or yesterday?

_____

_____

_____

_____

Pray for: Someone to be saved _____ someone to disciple _____

Date	Prayer Requests Received Today	How and when answered? (Come back and follow up as needed)

Week Twelve

Day: _____ Date: _____ Time: _____

Scripture Reading: I Corinthians 13:1-3

What did you learn in today's reading? How will you apply it to your life?

_____

_____

_____

_____

_____

_____

What must change in your life so that you are living as God wants?

_____

_____

_____

_____

_____

_____

What specific goal have you set for your Social/Emotional growth and refinement for this week? What is your progress?

_____

_____

Write the memory verse for this week: *1 Corinthians 15:57.*

_____

_____

_____

Write out three things you are grateful for today.

_____

_____

_____

Write out a prayer to God responding to today's lesson.

_____

_____

_____

_____

_____

_____

Ask, "Lord, what do You want to say to me personally about living out the most excellent way?"

_____

_____

_____

_____

_____

_____

Reflection: How did you experience God in a special way today or yesterday?

_____

_____

_____

_____

Pray for: Someone to be saved _____ someone to disciple _____

Date	Prayer Requests Received Today	How and when answered? (Come back and follow up as needed)

Week Twelve

Day: _____ Date: _____ Time: _____

Scripture Reading: I Corinthians 13:4-8a.

What did you learn in today's reading? How will you apply it to your life?

_____

_____

_____

_____

_____

_____

What area of love must change in your life, so you are living as God wants? How will you show it in your actions?

_____

_____

_____

_____

_____

_____

What specific goal have you set for your Physical growth and refinement for this week? What is your progress?

_____

_____

Write the memory verse for this week: *1 Corinthians 15:57.*

_____

_____

_____

Write out three things you are grateful for today.

_____

_____

_____

Write out a prayer to God responding to today's lesson.

_____

_____

_____

_____

_____

_____

Ask, "Lord, what do You want to say to me personally about love?"

_____

_____

_____

_____

_____

_____

Reflection: How did you experience God in a special way today or yesterday?

_____

_____

_____

_____

Pray for: Someone to be saved _____ someone to disciple _____

Date	Prayer Requests Received Today	How and when answered? (Come back and follow up as needed)

Week Twelve

Day: _____ Date: _____ Time: _____

Scripture Reading: I Corinthians 13:4b-13.

What did you learn in today's reading? How will you apply it to your life?

_____

_____

_____

_____

_____

_____

What must change in your life so that you are living in faith, hope, and love? How will you live it out?

_____

_____

_____

_____

_____

_____

What specific goal have you set for your Financial growth and refinement for this week? What is your progress?

_____

_____

Write the memory verse for this week: *1 Corinthians 15:57.*

_____

_____

_____

Write out three things you are grateful for today.

_____

_____

_____

Write out a prayer to God responding to today's lesson.

_____

_____

_____

_____

_____

_____

Ask, "Lord, what do You want to say to me personally about faith, hope, and love?"

_____

_____

_____

_____

_____

_____

Reflection: How did you experience God in a special way today or yesterday?

_____

_____

_____

_____

Pray for: Someone to be saved _____ someone to disciple _____

Date	Prayer Requests Received Today	How and when answered? (Come back and follow up as needed)

Notes

*I*n all things, God gets the victory, He makes the way. Depend on Him and wait for Him and praise Him.

"…Do not be afraid. Stand firm and you will see the deliverance the Lord will bring you today… The Lord will fight for you; you need only to be still."
– Exodus 14:13-14 NIV

Church Sermon Notes

Theme:

_____

_____

_____

Scriptures:

_____

_____

_____

Lessons:

_____

_____

_____

_____

_____

Application:

_____

_____

_____

_____

_____

Notes:

_____

_____

_____

_____

_____

Things to Remember from Week Twelve

Scriptures:

_____

_____

_____

Application:

_____

_____

_____

Goals Set:

_____

_____

_____

Memory Verse:

_____

_____

_____

Time with God:

_____

_____

_____

Reflection:

_____

_____

_____

Answered Prayers:

_____

_____

_____

Final Self-Evaluation

My life as of _____, 20_____

Spiritual	Yes	No	How Often
Do I read God's Word each day?			
Do I pray for my family, others, and myself?			
Am I attending a Bible-based Church?			
Do I testify about God to others?			
Mental			
Do I have a cheerful outlook?			
Do I listen to, watch, and read things that are uplifting and encouraging?			
Do I speak and react to others in a kind manner?			
Social/Emotional			
Do I honor and respect my spouse and family?			
Am I learning from a mentor or coach?			
Am I involved in a small group/community?			
Physical			
Do I eat/drink the right things each day?			
Do I exercise every day?			
Do I get enough rest daily?			
Financial			
Do I give to the Lord?			
Am I in debt?			
Do I save for an emergency fund?			
Total of columns			

Write what you are currently involved in doing. (Ex. Going to school, working at…, volunteering for…, names of close friends…, outdoor and indoor activities.)

_____

_____

_____

_____

_____

_____

_____

_____

_____

_____

_____

_____

_____

_____

_____

_____

_____

_____

_____

_____

_____

_____

_____

_____

_____

_____

_____

_____

Final Reflection

Take some time to reflect on key things that you learned that God revealed to you, or that you want to carry with you from this study.

_____
_____
_____
_____
_____
_____

Was there anything that seemed to be a repeating focus during each of the twelve weeks?

_____
_____
_____
_____
_____

In what ways have you grown in your relationship with God and recognizing His voice?

_____
_____
_____
_____
_____
_____

Once you've taken time to reflect on your journey, consider the questions in the Appendices to continue your journey and growth.

Appendix A
Accountability Questions for Women

Accountability works ONLY IF you are accountable.
http://www.characterthatcounts.org

1. When do you spend regular time in prayer?

2. Have your thoughts been pure? Have you resisted lustful, envious thoughts or exposed yourself to explicit materials?

3. How do you feel about how you have managed personal, family, and/or business finances?

4. What three relationships have you nurtured most?

5. What has made it difficult to do your 100% best in the different roles in your life?

6. Have your words built up or tore down others or self?
   Have you exposed yourself or contributed to gossip?
   Have you been committed to your words?
   Have you put yourself in a better light to those around you?

7. Do you feel you missed any opportunities to talk to people about the Lord?

8. Have you taken care of your body through daily physical exercise and proper eating/sleeping habits?

9. Which fruit of the Spirit (See Galatians 5:22-23) have you had the hardest time living out and why?

10. Have you left anything hidden in answering these questions?

Appendix B
Accountability Questions for Men

Accountability works ONLY IF you are accountable.
http://www.characterthatcounts.org

1. Have you spent daily time in the Scriptures and in prayer?

2. Have you had any flirtatious or lustful attitudes, tempting thoughts, or exposed yourself to any explicit materials, which would not glorify God?

3. Have you been completely above reproach in your financial dealings?

4. Have you spent quality relationship time with family and friends?

5. Have you done your 100% best in your job and/or school?

6. Have you told any half-truths or outright lies, putting yourself in a better light to those around you?

7. Have you shared the Gospel with an unbeliever this Session?

8. Have you taken care of your body through daily physical exercise and proper eating/sleeping habits?

9. Have you allowed any person or circumstance to rob you of joy?

10. Have you lied to us on any of your answers today?

Appendix C
Scripture Index

Week 1: "If you declare with your mouth, 'Jesus is Lord.' and believe in your heart that God raised him from the dead, you will be saved. For it is with your heart, that you believe and are justified, and it is with your mouth that you profess your faith and are saved...for everyone who calls on the name of the Lord will be saved" (Romans 10:9-10, 13).

Week 2: "But you will receive power when the Holy Spirit comes on you; and you will be My witness in Jerusalem, and in all Judea and Samaria, and to the ends of the earth" (Acts 1:8).

Week 3: "Keep this Book of the Law always on your lips; meditate on it day and night, so that you may be careful to do everything written in it. Then you will be prosperous and successful." (Joshua 1:8).

Week 4: "If we confess our sins, He is faithful and just, and will forgive us our sins and purify us from all unrighteousness" (I John 1:9).

Week 5: "Dear friends, now we are children of God, and what we will be, has not yet been made know. But we know that when Christ appears, we shall be like Him, for we shall see Him as He is. All who have this hope in Him purify themselves, just as He is pure" (I John 3:2-3).

Week 6: "So do not fear, for I AM with you; do not be dismayed, for I AM your God. I will strengthen you and help you; I will uphold you with My righteous right hand" (Isaiah 41:10).

Week 7: "For those who are led by the Spirit of God, are the children of God" (Romans 8:14).

Week 8: "Trust in the Lord with all your heart and lean not on your own understanding; in all your ways submit to Him, and He will make your paths straight" (Proverbs 3:5-6).

Week 9: "Until now you have not asked for anything in My name. Ask and you will receive, and your joy will be complete" (John 16:24).

Week 10: "This is the confidence we have in approaching God: that if we ask anything according to His will, He hears us. And if we know He hears us—whatever we ask—we know that we have what we asked of Him" (I John 5:14-15).

Week 11: "Do not conform to the pattern of this world but be transformed by the renewing of your mind. Then you will be able to evaluate and approve what God's will is –His good, pleasing, and perfect will" (Romans 12:2).

Week 12: "But thanks be to God! He gives us the victory through our Lord Jesus Christ (1 Corinthians 15:57).

References

Character that counts. (2005). Accountability questions for men. Retrieved from: www.characterthatcounts.org/accountqmensnew.html

Character that counts. (2005). Accountability questions for women. Retrieved from: www.characterthatcounts.org/accountqwomennew.html

Mathias, A. (2010) *Biblical Foundations of Freedom.* Anchorage, Alaska: Wellspring Ministries of Alaska.

Jeremiah, D. (2012) *One nation under God* [Prayer Guide]. www.NationalDayofPrayer.org

Virkler, M. (2005). *How to hear God's voice.* www.CWGministries.org

New International Version. (1991). The Life Application Study Bible. Tyndale House Publishers; Zondervan.

Notes

SCHOOL
OF THE SPIRIT

Three Powerful Benefits YOU Will Experience

1

You will learn to easily and daily hear God's voice

2

You will be able to live as Jesus did

3

You won't just study about God – you will have your own personal encounters with God

Take Your Place in God's Advancing Kingdom!

How far could you go with a Bible School in your pocket?

Go to: bwicministries.com/discipleship

Thank You!

Thank you so much for doing this Bible Study. I sincerely hope it has blessed you and impacted your life, your faith, and your intimacy with God. If so, give Him the glory, and would you help get it into more people's hands?

I would be so grateful if you shared with someone, and if you shared your honest review on the book page.

www.ingramcontent.com/pod-product-compliance
Lightning Source LLC
Chambersburg PA
CBHW082145120626

46553CB00010B/2765